MARKET
INTELLIGENCE

Withdrawn

MARKET RESEARCH IN PRACTICE SERIES

Published in association with The Market Research Society
Consultant Editors: David Barr and Robin J Birn

Kogan Page has joined forces with The Market Research Society (MRS) to publish this unique series, which is designed specifically to cover the latest developments in market research thinking and practice. Taking a practical, action-oriented approach, and focused on established 'need to know' subjects, the series will reflect the role of market research in the international business environment. This series will concentrate on developing practical texts on:

- how to use, act on and follow up research;
- research techniques and best practice.

Great effort has been made to ensure that each title is international in both content and approach and where appropriate, European, US and international case studies have been used comparatively to ensure that each title provides readers with models for research relevant to their own countries.

Overall the series will produce a body of work that will enhance international awareness of the MRS and improve knowledge of its Code of Conduct and guidelines on best practice in market research.

Other titles in the series:

Market Research in Practice: A guide to the basics, Paul Hague, Nick Hague and
  Carol-Ann Morgan
The Effective Use of Market Research, Robin J Birn

Forthcoming titles:

Questionnaire Design
Business to Business Market Research
Consumer Insight

To obtain further information, please contact the publisher at the address below:

Kogan Page Ltd
120 Pentonville Road
London N1 9JN
Tel: 020 7278 0433
www.kogan-page.co.uk

MARKET RESEARCH IN PRACTICE

MARKET INTELLIGENCE

HOW AND WHY ORGANIZATIONS USE MARKET RESEARCH

MARTIN CALLINGHAM

KOGAN PAGE

London & Sterling, VA

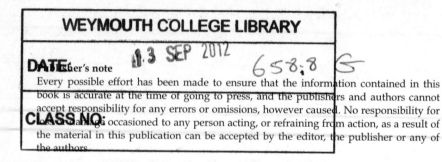
Publisher's note

Every possible effort has been made to ensure that the information contained in this book is accurate at the time of going to press, and the publishers and authors cannot accept responsibility for any errors or omissions, however caused. No responsibility for loss or damage occasioned to any person acting, or refraining from action, as a result of the material in this publication can be accepted by the editor, the publisher or any of the authors.

First published in Great Britain and the United States in 2004 by Kogan Page Limited

Apart from any fair dealing for the purposes of research or private study, or criticism or review, as permitted under the Copyright, Designs and Patents Act 1988, this publication may only be reproduced, stored or transmitted, in any form or by any means, with the prior permission in writing of the publishers, or in the case of reprographic reproduction in accordance with the terms and licences issued by the CLA. Enquiries concerning reproduction outside these terms should be sent to the publishers at the undermentioned addresses:

120 Pentonville Road
London N1 9JN
United Kingdom
www.kogan-page.co.uk

22883 Quicksilver Drive
Sterling VA 20166-2012
USA

© Martin Callingham, 2004

The right of Martin Callingham to be identified as the author of this work has been asserted by him in accordance with the Copyright, Designs and Patents Act 1988.

ISBN 0 7494 4201 8

British Library Cataloguing-in-Publication Data

A CIP record for this book is available from the British Library.

Library of Congress Cataloging-in-Publication Data

Callingham, Martin.
    Market intelligence: how and why organizations use market
    research/Martin Callingham.
        p. cm. -- (Market research in practice series)
    Includes bibliographical references and index.
    ISBN 0-7494-4201-8
    1. Marketing research I. Title: How and why organizations
    use market research. II. Title. III. Series.
    HF5415.2.C25 2004
    658.8'3--dc22

                                2004002672

Typeset by Datamatics Technologies Ltd, Mumbai, India
Printed and bound in Great Britain by Creative Print and Design (Wales), Ebbw Vale

Contents

The editorial board

CONSULTANT EDITORS

David Barr has been Director General of The Market Research Society since July 1997. He previously spent over 25 years in business information services and publishing. He has held management positions with Xerox Publishing Group, the British Tourist Authority and Reed International plc. His experience of market research is therefore all on the client side, having commissioned many projects for NPD and M&A purposes. A graduate of Glasgow and Sheffield Universities, David Barr is a Member of the Chartered Management Institute and a Fellow of The Royal Society of Arts.

Robin J Birn has been a marketing and market research practitioner for over 25 years. In 1985 he set up Strategy, Research and Action Ltd, which is now the largest international market research company for the map, atlas and travel guide sector, and the book industry. He is a Fellow of The Market Research Society and is also the editor of *The International Handbook of Market Research Techniques.*

ADVISORY MEMBERS

Professor Martin Callingham was formerly Group Market Research Director at Whitbread, where he ran the Market Research department for 20 years and was a non-executive director of the company's German restaurant chain for more than 10 years. Martin has also played his part in the market research world. Apart from being on many committees of the MRS, of which he is a Fellow, he was Chairman of the Association

Introduction

This is an unusual book because it is written from the client's perspective. This is important to the market research industry as, without client organizations, there would be no market research – it is they who generate it. Given this perspective, the book does not address the technical nature of market research (there are plenty of texts about this), nor does it look at advantages of doing it (there are many case studies to testify to this); rather it examines *how* market research occurs in client organizations.

Perhaps the single most important difference between working in the using side and the supplying side is that in the using side there is the constant need to be vigilant for 'dark forces' coming into play. Although market research is mostly done within organizations for straightforward logical reasons, there are occasions when much emotion surrounds it and the research may become the centre of a power struggle. It is when these comparatively rare situations arise that internal researchers either do their job or not, and dependent upon this the status of market research in the organization (and therefore the ability for this to have a positive impact on the business) is determined. Often it is possible to contain these types of problems before they become manifest, and doing this is one of the most important functions of a research manager. The 'power' and 'political' issues implicit in doing market research are always in the background and therefore are a reoccurring theme throughout this book.

A second theme that runs through this book is the one about the basic quantitative – qualitative divide. The natural tendency for business is to defer to numbers and to think that the world can be represented by them. Obviously to some extent this view is true, but it is not the whole truth. The belief in numbers leads businesses to prefer to work with quantitative research and only to accept qualitative research through necessity. Although the status of qualitative research has dramatically gained ground over the past years, it is still a fact that no major business decision is made on this alone. This book is unusual in that it positions qualitative and quantitative research on an equal footing, and explores, as a general theme, why this should be the case. In particular, it questions the reality of the notion of 'objective truth' that is often attributed to numerical representations.

The third theme that is omnipresent in the book is the difficulty of commissioning market research that is the right research for the company rather than for any one individual, as, among other reasons, failure to do this can lead to substantial 'pain' in the debrief. To help in understanding that there are many different 'takes' on most pieces of research the notion of 'research stakeholder' has been coined, as it is important to make quite sure that the various different perspectives are covered.

Chapter 1 examines the natures of commissioning organizations, and looks at the differences between commercial organizations (those that make money) and 'not for profit' organizations (those that spend money). The term 'research system' is defined as a way to examine the differences in the nature of research conducted by organizations of this type. The importance of brands to commercial organizations is discussed, and a new category of 'est' brands identified that, on the whole, do not need market research. Chapter 2 looks at the role of knowledge in an organization and positions it in the context of other assets. The chapter also discusses the role of creating an 'information climate' from the many disparate research projects (mostly of a short-term and tactical nature) that a company conducts. Chapter 3 looks at the way market research has an impact on the decision making of an organization and how this becomes more difficult as the size of the organization increases; this chapter also introduces the 'power' dimension in decision making. Chapter 4 examines the role of the market research function, and the debate that is taking place about consumer insight and the way that the market research function should be organized. Chapter 5 explores the buyer–supplier relationship and how business is placed. Chapters 6 and 7 address the issues surrounding the use of quantitative and qualitative information, especially the psychology of it, which is central to the research industry and to business's relationship to it. Chapter 8 is about the design of research and broadens the idea of what a 'design' is from being something that focuses on the *methodology* to be used to being something that focuses on the *process* that will be required to effect it. Chapter 9 is about how research is managed, from initially being a gleam in someone's eye to the eventual debrief. Chapter 10 discuses the ways that organizations react to the debrief, and Chapter 11 looks at the processes by which a company can address the issue of setting a future strategy. Finally, as a postscript, the whole 'story' that has been developed in the book is reviewed.

1 Types of organization

The market research that an organization commissions is very strongly related to the imperatives of that organization. This chapter examines the different types of organization that exist in order to lay the basis for the rest of this book. The fundamental divide is whether the purpose of the organization is to make money – that is, it is in the commercial sector – or whether it is to spend money – that is, it is in the 'not for profit' sector'. In practice, the great majority of research is commissioned by commercial organizations, but other types of organization are increasingly commissioning research. The largest of these is central government, followed by local government and the regulatory authorities. The differences between the commercial and 'not for profit' sectors are ones of orientation and ethos and these manifest themselves in the design of the market research that is commissioned. For this reason a new way of describing the 'research system' has been devised to help in understanding this.

KEY POINTS

- Organizations may be divided into those that operate for profit (commercial organizations), and those that do not ('not for profit' organizations). The latter group may be divided into the 'public sector' (gaining their finance at least in part from the public purse) and the rest.

■ Commercial organizations are driven by a need to show a surplus after satisfying the legitimate demands of their various business stakeholders (shareholders, employees, customers, local neighbourhood, and so on).

■ Public sector groups are spending public money and are under public scrutiny. They have a need to formulate effective policy and create ways of implementing it. They also need to judge the effectiveness of these actions and monitor the performance of the service that they provide. Market research is used in all these processes.

■ The imperatives of commercial and not-for-profit organizations are different, and are reflected in the way they use market research.

■ It is convenient to coin the phrase 'market research system' and use it to differentiate between the way organizations go about conceptualizing and doing their market research. The market research system comprises three separate parts: the market (the collection of what is being sold), the *research franchise* (consumers), and the research stakeholders (the people within the organization, or associated with it, that have an interest in the outcome of the research).

■ The research system of commercial organizations is comparatively simple, though it is well worth understanding the relative importance of the research stakeholders. The research franchise is rarely complicated, though it becomes more so for business-to-business research.

■ The research system for not-for-profit organizations is often more complicated than in commercial organizations. This is because the research stakeholders are often overlapping with the business stakeholders (which is rarely the case for commercial organizations), and they can often also become the object of research themselves (that is, part of the research franchise). This leads to more complex and larger-scale research in which the objectives multiply.

■ In government in the United Kingdom, there is a move to the principle of 'evidence based' policy, and consequently there is a requirement that the way the information has been gathered (on which this policy is based) should be available for external scrutiny. Obviously this puts more emphasis on the need for the methods used to clearly be of a suitable quality and fit-for-purpose.

COMMISSIONING ENVIRONMENTS

To understand how market research operates best, it is important to understand the interactions that it has with its commissioning environment. The major divide in organizational type is whether it is one that operates for profit (commercial organization) or one that does not (that is, organizations such as the government, institutions, charities and so on), although obviously organizations within each of these groups can vary greatly.

The great majority of commercial market research is actually done by commercial organizations, but not-for-profit ones do an increasing amount. As the dynamics of the commissioning of research has at its heart the way that an organization goes about making its decisions, and these can be fundamentally different between the commercial and not-for-profit environments, it is very important to understand the significant differences between them. The next two sections of this chapter examine these differences in detail.

COMMERCIAL ORGANIZATIONS

The need for profit

Commercial organizations have to make a profit. 'Profit' is an accountancy term describing what is left from the turnover after all the costs of running the organization have been met. Organizations have pressure to increase their profits, which they need in order to have the funds to reinvest in renewing and developing themselves. Profit is also taken as an indication of organizational health, and has an important role in making the organization attractive to investors: the other attraction is the presence of growth, or at least growth potential. Profit is therefore a fundamental driving force within commercial organizations.

Profit is not as simple as it seems

Whereas the turnover of a company is clearly defined and definite (the money comes in or it does not), the costs are often 'negotiable', and it is therefore possible to manage the level of profit a company declares in the short term. For example, the labour costs depend on the numbers of people employed and the pay they receive; by reducing both, the notional profit will increase. However, the long-term effect of doing this is to prejudice the effectiveness of the organization. This is true of all the 'cost lines' in the accounts, and companies have to choose how to spend their income to ensure that the long-term viability of the organization is balanced by the short-term requirement to show a surplus. This is generally referred to as the need to recognize that the organization has a number of business *stakeholders* whose legitimate needs have to be balanced one against the other. Typical business stakeholders are the employees, the shareholders, the customers, the suppliers, the local community and the legislature. Failure to get the balance right so that one group feels wrongly 'done by' results in that group's support being removed (cannot recruit good staff, customers stop buying and so on) and the ultimate failure of the company.

It is generally accepted that competitive pressure forces efficiency up – the company that sells at the lowest price and rewards its stakeholders the best is clearly onto a winning formula – but this is not easy to achieve. To achieve this a company has not only to be operating in the most efficient way, that is, not waste money, but also should be offering a product or service that is perceived to have greater value. When some form of extra value is attributed to the company's products, those products become brands.

Generation of value through brands

Chapter 2 considers in more detail the basic expression of assets in its various forms – especially that of knowledge – as a means of generating value. This section looks at the particular role that brands have in this (Aaker, 1996). The role of brands in creating the finance to run commercial companies can be very important, as the added value that they can bring helps to keep the different stakeholders happy. However, whether a product is a brand or not is not always clear, and the following sections describe one view about this and develop a way of segmenting brands that is helpful from the standpoint of whether they command market research or not.

Commodities

Initially, it is convenient to put the notion of brands in the context of a commodity. It is generally accepted that, in a commodity market, success only goes to the 'lowest cost producer'. Clearly, there is little room for manoeuvre – there can only be one lowest cost producer, and such companies have little room for marketing, let alone market research.

'est' brands

Commodity markets can, however, be thought of as segmenting into a first-level branding, which is to be the *best* in some form of simple and pragmatic way: for example, being the cheap*est*, the fast*est*, the most convenient(-*est*), the bigg*est* and so on. I have coined the term 'est' brand to describe this first-level segmentation of a market. This is the historic way of differentiating products, but of course there is again ultimately room for only one company in a particular sector to offer such a benefit. In practice, it is also not possible to deliver such a promise 100 per cent of the time. At a consumer level, brands of these types inevitably mean that there is some form of compromise in the offer in order to achieve the stated benefit, and consumer choice therefore depends on how an individual chooses to trade off the different elements of it. For example, 'It's the cheapest so I don't care that I have to travel a long way to get to it.'

The nature of the product promise of this type of brand is obvious and rarely, if ever, needs to be revisited, and market research therefore has a small role for organizations that are selling such brands. Communication costs can be quite low because of the obviousness of the positioning of the brand, and, indeed, companies that offer such brands can pride themselves on 'not advertising'. Furthermore, building and managing brands of this type depend almost exclusively on running the operations of the company better than the competitors, as this is the way to extract a benefit over and above the competition and thereby deliver the required profit. Consequently, such organizations tend to be very internally focused.

Added value brands

Brands can be created in an alternative way (Feldwick, 1996), where the value can come from the product being perceived to offer additional advantages at the psychological level (Levitt, 1981). This does not mean that the benefit is in any way less real to the purchaser of the product. A great deal of work (including substantial amounts of market research) has been done in trying to understand brand advantages of this type, and for good reason; the price that a person is prepared to pay for a relevant psychological advantage can be substantially above that of the basic cost of the product. This means that the opportunity of satisfying the competing, but legitimate, needs of the various stakeholders is more easily achieved and the long-term viability of the company ensured.

Brands of this type are not necessarily offering an obvious tangible or physical benefit, and therefore tend to have substantial communication costs. A major part of this cost is the advertising explaining the benefits of the offer, and it is not surprising that this also attracts substantial amounts of market research. Many would argue that it is the advertising that creates the brand, but this is not wholly true. A brand is more than advertising because, apart from its literal expression, it has a history, and consumers approach it in the light and experience of this. Meaning and significance also become attributed to it through its activities such as its sponsorship, its 'clothing', its promotional history, the 'company' it keeps and even the behaviour of the company behind it.

Commodity, 'est' brands and value added brands are different

Companies that are creating and developing added value brands are dealing with issues that are substantially more complicated than those that are selling a commodity or an 'est' brand. This means that they are organizationally different, and in particular will have larger and more developed marketing departments. Furthermore, they will need to be more consumer-centric, and have a real requirement to go out and talk to consumers or customers in a way that the others do not.

Therefore commercial organizations dealing with brands that are appealing to the psychological needs of a consumer group need to do market research, and typically they will research the whole gamut of the marketing mix, with particular emphasis on the brand itself and the advertising that supports it. Because of the need to ensure efficiency in each line of the accounts in terms of its ability to generate turnover, these organizations also tend to research the effectiveness of their marketing activities.

It is perhaps worth a word of caution here. The concept of an 'added value' type brand implies that the market will be segmented in terms of the consumers who are buying the brands. As such, 'targeting' – being an alignment between the brand's position and the needs of a particular consumer group – is 'good', and a prime notion that underwrites much market research is the concept of a loyal consumer attracted by, and satisfied by, his or her particular requirements being met by the brand. This is by no means a universally held truth (Anshuetz, 1997; Ehrenberg, Long and Kennedy, 2000).

NOT-FOR-PROFIT ORGANIZATIONS

Classification

Not-for-profit organizations have some profoundly different characteristics from commercial ones, but also some remarkable similarities. This leads to research that is commissioned in the not-for-profit sector having a number of differences from that commissioned by the commercial sector, although there are a lot of superficial similarities. Once this has been said, the imperatives of the two sides are getting nearer to one another – mostly driven by the need to be more conscious about value for money.

There are a number of different types of not-for-profit organization. They may be divided into two broad groups, public sector organizations, and not-for-profit organizations that lie outside the public sector.

Public sector organizations include:

- representational organizations (such as central and local government);
- regulatory authorities;
- public bodies (such as health authorities, educational organizations, the cultural service industry and so on);
- institutions such as museums and art galleries.

Those that are non-profit-making but lie outside the public sector include:

- 'lobbying' organizations (such as charities);
- those that are concerned with looking after their members' interests (such as the professional societies, the 'mutuals' and unions);
- political parties.

Although the differences between these groups will be examined shortly, it is important to recognize that the big not-for-profit players in research are central government, followed by the local authorities and regulatory authorities.

Naturally the actions of these different groups overlap (as indeed they do with commercial organizations), but the organizational intent is different in each case, and this affects how they operate and, at the level of this book, the role that market research has in them.

Representational organizations

Central government

Governments are run by politicians who propose to run the country according to their ideology and election promises. Being human, they also have an eye on winning the next election. Government policies are effected through the means of the various governmental departments, which are populated by career civil servants and led by political appointees. Government undertakes considerable amounts of research, but the stakeholders are varied. The interests of politicians and civil servants may not be the same. Those in the government hierarchy are seeking association with a successful initiative and hopeful of promotion, while those in the Civil Service are interested in being seen to have been professional and have spent public money wisely.

The nature of the research that takes place on behalf of central government is very diverse, covering virtually all conventional research types. However, the background psychology often can be very different, and this also differs across the various research stakeholders. Because of the importance of the central government sector to the research industry, it is worthwhile examining different types of research that take place in this sector.

Fundamental to central government are the policies that it pursues. The degree to which the ideology of the party in power impacts on a particular policy will vary a great deal: for example health, education and fiscal policies tend to be strongly influenced by the party's ideology, but for instance, the future of broadcasting might not. In cases of the latter type, the formulation of policy may involve an extensive consultation exercise that could include formal market research. Policy research, if done, may well influence the nature of the policy adopted. For example, in 1988 the Broadcasting Standards Council was created and was required to draw up a code of practice to include standards of taste and decency: research had an obvious role in helping this (Docherty and Morrison, 1990).

The move towards evidence-based policy has been increasing

recently in the UK. In 1999 a government spokesman wrote: 'Social Science should be at the heart of policy-making. We need a revolution in relations between government and the social research community – we need social scientists to help us determine what works and why. What types of policy initiatives are likely to be most effective' (Rigg, 2003). This is a pretty fundamental shift and is probably an indication of the way that the United Kingdom is being influenced by the liberal socialist tradition of the European Union as much as by the orientation of the government that wrote it.

Policy research can be used to help formulate policy presentation, often in the form of television advertising. Examples of this are public awareness programmes to encourage a particular behaviour, for example, campaigns about drug misuse, drink driving, fire risk, opportunities for grants and so on, and naturally a government minister will be also interested in knowing the degree to which such campaigns are effective. The civil servants who were involved in getting these campaigns up and running will be more interested in ensuring that these campaigns are comprehensible to their target audience and cost effective in achieving their objectives. Research into advertising can therefore be thought of in very different ways by the various research stakeholders.

Government will also want to check out whether a policy is being effectively implemented, and where the implementation scheme could be improved. The Civil Service (or other groups, such as local authorities, depending upon the policy) takes the brunt of this and is expected to show success through the measurements against targets for specified performance indicators. Increasingly, the targets are set in terms of 'hard' (behavioural) measures, although market research clearly also has a role.

Ultimately, government will also want to know whether the whole scheme is misplaced and whether, no matter how well it is implemented, it would have no or little effect.

Government departments produce a great number of forms that citizens are expected to fill in on different occasions. These forms deal with the complexities and exceptions that have been introduced through Parliament, and have to be understood by a wide range of people of diverse backgrounds and literary skills. Research is clearly important in helping make possible what many might think is impossible!

One of the features of open government is that the process of procurement has to be seen to be fair and open, which tends to make it more laborious, time consuming and therefore also more expensive. This is considerably different from the commercial sector, which tends (perhaps wrongly: see Chapter 5) not to be concerned with such matters. As policy is to be based on the output of the research, another aspect of open government is that the method of the research should be able to stand up to external gaze and be clearly fit-for-purpose (Rigg, 2003). This represents another difference between research undertaken by government and that undertaken by the private sector.

Local government

Local authorities (colloquially known as 'the councils') are responsible for local administration in the United Kingdom and are elected bodies. They have been required by government to improve their processes of public consultation via issuing a series of consultation papers (in 1998), and have been asked to consider a variety of methods including such non-traditional ones as citizens' panels and juries (Lewis and White, 1999). In particular this has been aimed at improving turnout at local elections, or at least ensuring that the local population's needs and concerns are genuinely being understood, and to make up for what is referred to as the 'democratic deficit'. This has led to a tendency for research to be very widespread in terms of the sample construction (the local authority wishes to be seen to be inclusive) and often local authorities refer to research as a 'public consultation exercise'.

Since the 1980s, local authorities have been required to obtain the lowest cost through competitive tendering. More recently, this policy has been acknowledged as causing a degradation in services, and to compensate for this the notion of 'best value' has been accepted. Councils can now avoid the need for competitive tendering if they can show that their services offer best value. This may be established through financial analysis or by formal market research. (Mattinson, 1998). The net effect of this has meant that research for local authorities has grown rapidly in recent years (Lovell and Henderson, 2000).

The worlds of government at the central and local levels are really quite different from that of the commercial sector for all the reasons already given. The emphasis is that the former is predicated on the leaders seeking to win the next election, while in commercial organizations, the requirement is to achieve good profit performance and share growth. There are also differences between these representational groups and other public bodies, as will be discussed below.

Regulatory bodies

In the United Kingdom there are many bodies that have been set up by government to monitor a number of industries where the normal forces of consumerism may be muted, or where a greater good other than the simple profit imperative needs to be taken into account. Among these are the Financial Services Authority (FSA), the Audit Commission, OFCOM and the Competition Commission. These bodies often commission extensive research to help them reach their conclusions. These bodies are representational in that they purport to speak for the users of services.

Other public bodies

There are a number of public bodies concerned with public sector service provision such as the health authorities, education (Robson and Ballard, 2000) and the police, which tend to be locally based and accountable through a variety of boards or committees. Such organizations need to show that they are legitimate custodians of public money, and like the local authorities will tend to go through a series of consultation exercises.

Institutions and the heritage cultural industries

There is a whole area of the public sector that is now described as the 'cultural heritage industry'. In the United Kingdom, this includes such entities as the National Trust and English Heritage (responsible for preserving the countryside and historic buildings), which are generally set up for a particular purpose and receive public money to help them achieve it. The theatre, arts and museums also frequently receive government grants. They are not so different from the generality of public bodies but they are usually more remote from the political dimension, although at any time they can suddenly become a focus. There probably is, however, increasing politicization of institutions. For example, institutions such as art galleries and museums are now expected to provide a broader-based public service as well as being the custodians of scholarship and aesthetic appreciation (Fisher, 2000). Consequently, these organizations may use research to show that the way they have set about doing it is acceptable to the public, and that targets they have set are being achieved. This transformation can be a traumatic change for long-established and sometimes inward-looking cultures, and research can have an important impact in helping the culture to adjust to its new imperatives. They may even use research to develop their product too, and in this case they will tend to use research for straightforward and easy-to-understand reasons. Such institutions are now more likely to invest in marketing and to employ people to do it. This change will automatically generate more of the sort of market research that commercial organizations do.

Membership organizations

Membership organizations exist to further the interests of their members. Examples of these are trade unions, professional societies, mutual societies and trusts. In general these organizations are not heavily involved in research, and when they occasionally engage in it, it is to help formulate policy with respect to development of the organization, or the provision of membership services. These organizations tend to be naive research users and can require a lot of hand-holding by their suppliers, both in having realistic expectations of the output of the research and in actually translating it into some form of decision.

Fund-raising organizations

These organizations are generally charities and are involved in fund-raising to finance a 'good cause' activity. Unlike commercial organizations they do not need to display a profit at the end of the year, but they do need to finance themselves as well as spend money on their primary interest. Their orientation is therefore not that different from a commercial organization and it is arguable that they need to build brands in the same way. However, they are not generally looked at in this manner nor do they conceptualize themselves in this way. At the heart of the fundraising activity will be the belief that their claim for money is of particular value and importance. Consequently, evidence of this becomes an important issue and research can help in substantiating it. Larger charities engage in fund-raising marketing campaigns, and research can help in how best to formulate the message such that it is understandable and impactive; they may well also wish to check the efficacy of their marketing with a view to learning how to develop its effectiveness. In a number of cases, a charity can have been around for many years and the need that it was originally set up to help has changed in nature. This can lead the organization to having to reposition itself to better address the contemporary situation. This means that classic brand repositioning work needs to be done, and research has its ordinary commercial role in this.

Political parties

A political party's 'product' is its policies. The nature of political parties is that their policies tend to be ideological and therefore the very basis on which they seek to obtain power. In addition, the so-called 'democratic nature' of political organizations implies that there will have been many debates before arriving at the policies, and therefore formal research of them is not necessary. A political party has the prime requirement of getting and staying elected. Therefore its need for research tends to be heavily weighted to understanding the best way of *presenting* a policy (rather than in developing its actual contents), and, then, after it has been implemented (if the party is in power), of presenting the *outcome* of it in successful terms (Mattinson and Bell, 2000). Commonly, this process is called 'putting a spin on it'.

Summary of not-for-profit organizations

The not-for-profit sector is a complex sector that is increasingly using research. It ranges from the extremely professional buying and using of research to the quite amateur, and the research supplier needs to recognize the difference in sophistication that exists in this sector compared with what is normally encountered in the commercial sector. It is also often the case that people working in the not-for-profit sector, especially the smaller organizations, tend to be genuinely committed to the cause they are working for and demonstrate a great enthusiasm for it. They can project this enthusiasm onto all the people that work and surround them, with the consequence that they can be very demanding in their expectations, especially with respect to what they get for their money. Perhaps more important is the difference of orientation of the entire not-for-profit sector from the commercial sector, which gives a different emphasis to its research requirements because the social climate and politics in which research is done are different.

The research system

In order to understand the dynamics of the research process in an organization, it is convenient to coin the term *research system* to describe the combination of the *market* (what is being 'sold'), the collection of people who have an interest in the research output (the *research stakeholders*) and those who are being researched (the *research franchise*). These terms have been used informally in the text of this chapter, but it will now be helpful to define them more rigorously, and each will be dealt with in turn.

The market

The *market* is the collection of things (products) that are to be sold and bought, and what this means is self-evident in commercial organizations. However, as marketing becomes a more generally understood and accepted function, some of its concepts are spreading and the meaning of the term is broadening. So, for example, it would be normal to talk about the 'market' of a series of employment benefits when a human resources (personnel) manager is doing research into these among employees or potential employees.

In the not-for-profit sector there will also be some form of 'thing' that is the object of the research and that, when summed up, becomes the equivalent of the market. This could be, for example, the number of people who have taken up a benefit, or are aware of a social programme, such as the need to fit fire alarms, or have a defined attitude to hard drug taking. At a more abstract level is the concept of the market for a policy or a belief, meaning those who are interested, or potentially interested in it: charities are often interested in such markets.

This means that increasingly, the commercial and not-for-profit sectors are not differentiated much in this aspect of the research system. However, this is not the case for the other two dimensions, as will now be shown.

The research stakeholders

The *research stakeholders* are those people who have an interest in the output of the research, and in commercial research they are generally different from the *business stakeholders* (shareholders, employees, customers and so forth). The research stakeholders in commercial organizations normally include the various levels of the marketing department and the agencies it employs – typically an advertising agency – but there are often other business functions that may be interested such as R&D, production, the sales force, or the board itself. In general, research will be commissioned by just one of these stakeholders, but in many cases some of the other stakeholders, who are often in the background, can be very influential in the conception and utilization of the research and therefore should not be ignored.

Obviously there are analogous research stakeholders in the not-for-profit sector. These could be various parts of the hierarchy, other parts of government and agencies that are involved in advising or implementing some aspect of the programme, and to this extent the commercial and not-for-profit sectors are similar to one another. However, there are often additional stakeholders present in the not-for-profit sector case whose presence can further complicate the research process if their presence is not properly appreciated and their interests included. For example, in the case of NHS work additional research stakeholders might be patients, GPs and internal staff .

The orientation of the various research stakeholders in either sector affects, to a considerable degree, how the research is designed and how the output of it will end up being used. Consequently, it is important that this should be taken into account when the research is being designed and debriefed. Failure to do this is often one of the most important reasons that a piece of market research can be seen to have failed (see Chapter 8).

The research franchise

The *research franchise* consists of those people who have an interest in the market and become the target for the research – the respondents. In most cases of research, the research franchise is obvious and hardly gets a second thought, but who is researched will determine what is found out. Typical samples used for research are the users of a product or a nationally represented sample of people in the United Kingdom, but it can be more complicated than this. A not uncommon debate in commercial sector research, for example, could be whether consideration should be given to separating those who buy for their own consumption and those who buy for others to consume. Furthermore, the research franchise can actually be different for different stakeholders in some research: for example, in issues about the relationship between the manufacturer, the retailer and the ultimate consumer. Marketing people will be interested in talking to the ultimate consumer, while the account managers will want to talk to their customers, who may well be intermediaries along the distribution chain. The research franchise of these two potential stakeholders is different, yet the apparent purpose of the research could be the same.

This now takes us into the realms of business-to-business research, where businesses are selling to businesses. Here the concept of the decision-making unit (DMU) is quite well developed (that is, how the different people or functions relate to one another in coming to a decision about a purchase), and this is clearly a very important dynamic to understand. The research franchise in this case is difficult to define – who exactly wields the power to decide to buy or not, and how do the various elements of the DMU interrelate?

In the case of not-for-profit organizations, there will generally be a fairly obvious target group to research, just as there is in commercial market research, but the franchise is equally often much wider. This is because citizens have a stake in the society as a whole and might feel very strongly about a particular thing, even if it does not impact directly on them. Aspects such as fairness, rights, needs, public good and other moral dimensions may come strongly into play (Hedges and Duncan, 2000), and including this in the research design increases the diversity of the research franchise.

SUMMARY OF DIFFERENCES BETWEEN THE COMMERCIAL AND NOT-FOR-PROFIT SECTORS

The primary difference between the two sectors is the orientation of the organizations with respect to money. In the case of commercial organizations there is a need to make a surplus, while in the not-for-profit organizations there is a need to spend it (wisely, hopefully). This leads to a fundamental difference in the orientation of the two types of organization. However, once that has been said there is a lot in common between them, and this commonality is getting stronger, not weaker. The differences can best be illustrated by thinking about the nature of the stakeholders and the fact that they may well be interested in different research franchises.

It should be apparent from all the above that issues of research design, especially in terms of the sample and possibly in terms of the orientation of the research objectives (and hence the questions asked), are ultimately dependent on having a clear conception of the research system that applies. This will be developed later in Chapter 8.

CONCLUSION

Commercial organizations provide the bedrock for the market research industry, but in the United Kingdom government is not far behind. The various organizational types described in this chapter have a very different *raison d'être*, and therefore the research that they commission, though seemingly similar, is operating under very different imperatives. The criteria for judging whether a piece of research has been successful can therefore be quite different, and considerable care has to be taken to ensure that these factors are taken into account at both the design and debriefing stages of the research.

2 Knowledge is the most important asset of a company

Organizations, especially commercial organizations (which this chapter is mostly about) must have an eye on their value. Ultimately, what constitutes 'value' has to be the market view, simply because value is a financial term. However, what lies behind the value of a company is a subject of some debate, and there are quite diverse views about the answer. The importance of this debate is that a proper conception of the basis of the financial value of a company allows for the proper management of it. This chapter examines the various ways in which the value of a company can be described, and looks at the most contemporary expression of this, which is that the greatest asset of a company is its knowledge. Market research is an important way in which a company builds its knowledge, especially about the brands it has and the markets it trades in, and therefore the role of knowledge in company value is important to understand, in order to appreciate the ultimate purpose for conducting market research.

KEY POINTS

- There are many ways of assessing the *value* of a company, but ultimately these stems from the knowledge that it has.
- Market research is an important way in which the knowledge of a company grows.
- Knowledge is conceptualized as 'explicit' (codified) and 'tacit' (codifiable, but not yet codified). More recently, the term 'tacit knowledge' is being used to describe the type of knowledge that is *soft* and *conceptual*.
- Organizations are increasingly trying to manage their knowledge, and do it through two types of route: the *mechanical route*, relying on a heavyweight IT infrastructure, and the *organic* route, which attempts to use cultural management methods. It seems that both methods are required for there to any chance of success.
- The majority of organizations are *doing* entities and *effect* processes. Numbers are used to evaluate and justify change in the organization, and this attracts a particular type of person to the organization. Things that can be expressed as numbers are obviously easily codifiable, and organizations work basically with explicit information.
- ISO 9000 is a quality system that seeks to grow the organization's knowledge through identifying the information that it needs in order to operate, which is as yet not explicit. This basically denies the importance of the role of conceptual information in the running of an organization.
- The decisions with which organizations are faced are becoming more complex, and there is a growing need for them to work in a more conceptual way. This means that there has been a growth in the type of market research that feeds this type of information, namely qualitative research, and a more intuitive use in general of the different elements of knowledge to gain insight. This has fuelled the growth of customer or consumer insight groups.

COMPANY VALUE AND EARNING POWER

The value of a company is what people will be prepared to pay for it. This is expressed as the *market value* of the company, which for a quoted company is the value that the stock market collectively puts on the shares. This market value is related mostly to the current and future potential earning capability of the company, adjusted for the risk involved in the particular business and the sector that it is in. The market value of the company may be greater, the same, or less than the money that has been invested in it. This discrepancy arises because the calculation that leads to company valuation does not directly take this investment into account, only the *consequence* of the investment.

The money that has been invested in the company ends up as fixed assets (such as factories), assets that are required to fuel the business (raw materials, unsold stock), and liquid assets (cash and investments). These assets, minus what the company owes, comprise the capital employed, which is often used for earnings efficiency calculations: for example, return on capital employed (Hitching and Stone,1988).

If the company is inefficiently run, its returns will be low for its sector, and it will carry a lower market value. This is easy to understand. But sometimes a company may return a higher figure than expected, and this is more difficult to understand.

One way of looking at this is to imagine that the company has some other 'assets', which are adding extra earnings to it above what would be expected by the efficient utilization of the capital employed. The value of these 'hidden' assets can, of course, easily be calculated from the difference in actual earnings from those that would be expected. But this is mathematical fudge; there must be something that is causing this extra income to be generated. So what could these hidden assets be, for which value can be ascribed?

DIFFERENT TYPES OF ASSET

Although the asset value of a company is clearly closely financially defined, it has become conventional to use the term 'asset' in a more general way. The following examines different types of asset that a company might perceive that it has.

Asset value of brands

More recently there has been a recognition that companies may have a greater value than they appear to have because they own brands, which themselves have become tradable items. The ownership of brands is just one aspect of the potential future earnings of the company, so it has always been taken implicitly into account, but more companies are explicitly valuing their brands and some are including them on their balance sheets. In small companies, this used to be talked about in terms of 'goodwill'. The idea of adding brands to the balance sheet seems to be fading at the moment, but it is philosophically interesting to consider brands as hidden assets, because their very purpose is to be something that can command a higher price than its stated worth.

Exclusivity

Some companies have value because they own non-tangible assets, such as trading agreements or patent rights: that is, the legal right to do something that others cannot do, which effectively gives them some form of monopoly. These intellectual rights are also formally recognized as having value. Other companies may have secret processes which, while not legally protected, are not available to others, and therefore allow them to do things that others cannot.

Customers

The last few years have seen the idea that the customers of a company are a strong asset. This has led to the growth in the ideas behind customer relationship management, or CRM as it is known. Customer relation management argues that attention should be paid particularly to those few customers that provide the majority of the company's business. Although it is obvious that this truth has always been known to small businesses, in classic consumer businesses there are obviously far too many customers for anyone to know individually. However, now it is possible to 'know' them through the medium of a database holding information about them. This database is potentially of great value to the company and, for that matter, to its competitors.

A whole philosophy has now grown up around CRM, which at its worst seems to treat customers as unthinking objects that must be stimulated in some perverse Pavlovian way. It is based on collecting data about customers at each point of contact that they have with the organization, and storing it for analysis and for formulating marketing.

When it is done well it can build good and lasting relationships between a company and a customer – but we have all experienced this being done badly. There is substantial literature about this, and many case studies have been described, but common experience suggests that successful CRM is still a rarity.

Employees

In the last 10 years or so, it has become more common for companies to talk about their employees as being their greatest asset. Generally these companies are in the service industries, and this comment links to current ideas of customer service. Early ideas of customer service produced a world where staff were expected to act like some form of robot ('Have a nice day'), or answer the phone in three rings and say 'Can you hold?'. It is now generally recognized that staff service comes from liberating staff members to act naturally and giving them the power (empowering them) to do the sensible thing. This is extremely hard to do in practice, and the approach that is now mostly proposed is to set up a culture with values from which the staff can draw, bringing about coherence and consistency in behaviour which is not contrived or false. This is what naturally happens in small businesses where the staff takes their lead from the owner; it is, of course, much harder for a large company.

Culture

Cultural management has been seen as a way of aligning the objectives of the employees and improving their effectiveness through building a collaborative environment. Ultimately this is all about leadership and inspiration, to which financial heads of companies are not especially attitudinally attuned or sympathetic, and with very few exceptions, it proves extremely difficult to effect within a company. It is also very expensive in terms of the staff time required to do the training, and the training itself is not cheap. The basic belief was that it should be possible to get a self-sustaining positive cultural environment where new joiners would inevitably assume the company values, or leave if they found they could not. Until recently, companies often held a substantial proportion of their employees for a long time, especially those in more senior positions. In such cases, the possibility of achieving a self-sustaining culture is possible in principle. However, flexible employment is increasingly becoming the norm, and indeed the whole notion of what a corporation actually is seems to be changing. Consequently, it seems likely that cultural management will become increasingly difficult to achieve within corporations, as employee turnover rates increase and the 'contractor' society grows.

KNOWLEDGE AS THE ULTIMATE ASSET

There is a common theme that runs through the previously described ideas of what a broad view of a company's assets are (brands, exclusivity of trading rights, customers, staff or culture), and this is the notion that *knowledge* itself is an asset to a company. Indeed, it could be said that the very existence of a particular body of knowledge (within an organization) is unique and is what ultimately separates a company from its competitors, for good or bad. Viewing the assets of a company in this way is obviously very important from the standpoint of suppliers of market research – for they are providing part of the very essence of what the company is.

Types of knowledge

Recently, there has been a lot of attention paid to the idea of knowledge management (Martensson, 2000). An important separation has been made between the concepts of *explicit* knowledge (that which is codified and written down) and *tacit* knowledge (that which is simply assumed, and lives within the people or the very culture of the organization). The term 'tacit knowledge' originally seems to have meant literally things that were concrete but not yet codified. However, the term now seems to be broadening in meaning and changing its focus, to refer increasingly to the more abstract and conceptual type of knowledge.

Functions within organizations deal predominantly with one of these types of knowledge. As some people are happy working with the concrete and absolute while others are happier with the abstract and the conceptual, people will naturally gravitate to those functions that operate in the knowledge domain with which they feel happiest. As organizations are *doing* entities, this means that commercial businesses are on the whole populated with people who are happiest with explicit knowledge. This has a profound effect on the way market research is commissioned, thought about and used, particularly the issue of the quantitative/qualitative divide (see Chapters 6 and 7).

The meaning of the concept of 'knowledge' is a philosophical point, and words such as: 'facts', 'information', 'knowledge', 'insight', 'wisdom' and so on have been bandied around for years. However, it is convenient to think of a variety of categories such as the 'factualness' of the information (its intrinsic ambiguity as distinct from its accuracy), relationships between facts (which could be strong or simply loose constellations of ideas), empirical processes (that is, 'this works' – now called 'best practice'), thoughts, ideas and hunches.

MANAGEMENT OF KNOWLEDGE

Companies have always attempted to manage their knowledge, and have historically seen it as comprising the variety of skills, contacts and the general 'nous' that they had. So there is nothing new in the ideas behind knowledge management. However, what is new is that the volume of information has grown substantially in the last few years, and computer technology has developed to a degree which, in principle, should allow this information to be better handled. In addition, communication is now much better, so that knowledge (if it has value) travels around more effectively, and the competitive advantage it gave is quickly eroded.

Certain established quality systems such as ISO 9000 attempt to convert the tacit knowledge of an organization into the explicit. ISO 9000 was created to help organizations reduce the failure rate in the delivery of a promised specification. Such failure was identified generally as arising from the inconsistent use of tacit knowledge used in the original meaning of the term (that is, literal information that was not as yet codified). ISO 9000 involves specifying the output desired (goods' quality), writing out all the procedures that are needed to be followed to achieve this specification, and installing tracking systems to ensure that the written procedures are followed. By ensuring that, for any given item, the procedures had indeed been followed, and by checking that the item met the specification, it follows that if on any particular occasion, it did not (that is, it 'non-conformed'), then there must be something missing from the written procedures. A detailed investigation into the reasons behind the non-conformity therefore should allow for this missing procedure to be identified, and for yet another bit of tacit information to be made explicit, and hence the knowledge base of the organization to grow.

Total Quality Management (TQM) systems have been very effective in manufacturing environments, but although there is no reason these systems should not be just as effective in other environments, in practice they do not seem to have been so. However, it is notable that the places where TQM has not been so effective are more likely to have tacit information of the modern conception (that is, conceptual information) than are manufacturing companies, where the older version of the meaning of tacit information (uncoded explicit information) is more likely to apply.

There are, however, some more fundamental and psychological reasons to explain the lower success rate in non-manufacturing environments. Arguably individuals do not want their particular knowledge to be made explicit as it reduces their perceived importance and sense of personal identity within the organization. This is hardly a surprising phenomenon as it is a historically recognized way by which groups and guilds (now professional bodies) have preserved their distinctiveness and earning power. Unfortunately, these factors still seem to be undercurrents in moderating the effects of knowledge management systems.

Mechanical knowledge management

Management of knowledge (often abbreviated to KM) can take two forms. The first form is the elaborate 'library route' using computer-based systems to capture and help collate disparate pieces of information (both internal and external), and to automatically feed relevant information pointers to groups of people that the system has identified within the organization.

The sharing of information by common interest groups is an important aspect of knowledge management, and the very definition of these interest groups is itself an added advantage. This is because the members of these groups then know who in the organization has similar interests, and they can therefore directly contact each other when they are seeking the solution to particular aspects of their problems.

Although the creation of these computer-generated people networks is an outcome of some of these systems, structurally they draw on the mechanical analogy of a spider's web, rather than a more fluid ecological model to be described later. At their worst, these mechanical management systems are little more than a collection of databases with a search engine. Inevitably, this route involves very heavy IT investment, and they are generally manifest tangibly as a corporate intranet. However, their provision has again not seemed to bring the success that was hoped for. This may be because too much is expected from installing software that the providers strangely describe as 'software solutions', when logically this installation is only the first stage of introducing knowledge management systems into a company. In practice, it seems that such systems are information management systems, rather than real knowledge management systems.

Organic knowledge management

The second way of managing knowledge is *cultural*, and involves finding useful summarizing rules that are easy to identify with and to use. Structurally this draws on ideas that have been developed in understanding ecological systems, and can be thought of as being 'organic' rather than 'mechanical'. There seems to be general recognition that the organic approach has to be present as well as the technological one in order to breath life into the sharing of knowledge, but it is, of course, much less easy and more time consuming to implement.

The whole of this area of knowledge management is difficult because it is all-encompassing and the boundaries of it are distinctly fuzzy. There is, therefore, a danger that the notion of 'knowledge management' will become so diffuse and general that it ceases to have useful conceptual meaning. For this reason it is easier to think about separate knowledge *domains*, and in this book the area of particular interest is the domain that surrounds marketing.

Customer relationship management

As described in Chapter 1, some organizations take the view that their customers are their most important assets. At the ultimate level, this involves managing the relationship through monitoring customers' behaviour at every point where they have contact with the organization, and supplementing this with additional information about them wherever possible: for example, via list purchase, modelling and so on. By these means, the organization attempts to construct individual marketing plans for each customer, with a view to retaining its customers or, preferably, taking more money off them in the face of competition. This effectively means proactively engaging with the customer and being able to respond in a knowledgeable way when the customer has contacted the organization. Clearly, with all this codified customer behaviour on a database, it is possible to do clever analysis – but see Chapter 6 for the inherent weaknesses in this.

In this world, where customer information is taken seriously, it is to easy (but misguided) to imagine that information about customers comprises part of the knowledge of the company, and therefore customer relationship management systems and knowledge management systems are sometimes spoken of in the same breath. This can be particularly the case when the customers are primarily other businesses (Adams, 2000).

DEVELOPING AN INFORMATION CLIMATE FOR MARKETING

In marketing there is a lot of explicit knowledge about how to conduct the process of marketing (or at least that is what marketing proponents would like us all to believe). However, there is also an enormous amount of tacit knowledge about the market in question, the brands themselves and how people relate to them. Much of this tacit knowledge is prejudicial and frankly wrong, being based on home psychology, yesterday's information and what it might be expedient to say to cloud an issue. Such statements of 'fact' (often very plausible) are not readily refuted and are actually cultural myths. Similarly, incorrect beliefs and misconceptions exist in the not-for-profit sector.

Market research is conducted generally through the medium of projects with quite closely specified outcomes. These tight specifications are to help with particular decisions which are, on the whole, short-term tactical decisions. The very tightness of the specification can itself act to prevent real knowledge being created (Cowan, 1994) because the new information might be collected within the myopic straitjacket of incorrect hypotheses and cultural myths (see Chapter 8). Occasionally large-scale projects are undertaken, but their output is so extensive that it can be difficult for individuals to get their heads around it in the time they are prepared to give to it. So the pool of tacit knowledge does not become explicit, and there is a real danger that the myriad projects make the situation more confused, not less.

It is, however, possible for information to progressively become enriched as project feeds on project, but this depends upon the company's attitude to it. If an organization believes that it really wants to be people focused (which most seem to say these days) then the organization's consumer and market information requirements (or the various not-for-profit equivalents) need to be managed as a coherent whole (Nonka, and Takeeuchi, 1995). This should be the real job of an in-house market or social research group.

Unfortunately there are moves against this. For example, the in-house market research function can easily reduce to being an expert buying group, which, given the quality of the research industry in general, would not seem to be necessary or to add value (see Chapter 4). In addition, there is a trend to fragment such in-house research groups across the various functions or brand groups, where they become 'closer to their customers' and can provide a more integrated view of the market. This can be a positive move, but can also lead to problems when the different brand groups are working in the same markets. This is because, in these circumstances, it is possible for different conceptions of the market to develop within the same organization. This may not matter too much at the brand level, but makes establishing a coherent market strategy for the entire company very difficult.

The management of the tacit market and people information of an organization is about having shared assumptions at the highest level. The properties of a coherent information climate that result when this happens are quite clear (Callingham, 1991). Conversations about the system can be held at a more sophisticated level without the basic assumptions being challenged, and therefore are more profound. It is possible for an individual to hold heretical views, as these are more easily managed in an environment that has confidence in its information climate, and these types of non-conforming views are a source of regeneration and development of the whole information climate. The ability of individuals to collaborate is bettered through this alignment of knowledge, and ideas are more easily surfaced, fostered and developed. Furthermore, the decision that one person or group makes is intelligible to another, and the decision-making processes move more smoothly. Good quality information climates do not need to be holistically logically consistent, and so do not become a straitjacket to thinking, but rather a liberation of it.

All this is idealistic, of course, but there is some evidence that it can occur in large organizations, and definite evidence that it exists in small ones.

CONCLUSION

Although the assets of an organization are quite clear in financial terms, the extrapolation of this idea into other domains seems to have been fruitful. The current situation is that there is a strong belief that knowledge is the ultimate asset of an organization, and that this knowledge divides into three broad types: concrete explicit knowledge; the knowledge that could become explicit if it were to be sought out; and a more diffuse conceptual knowledge. The management of knowledge is therefore increasingly being recognized as very important. There seem to be two opposing approaches to it: effectively one that believes that computing-led systems are sufficient, and the other that thinks they may be necessary but are not in themselves sufficient, requiring additional work at the cultural level to liberate the mechanical system's potential. Unfortunately, cultural management is difficult, and made harder by the increasing mobility of labour arising as a result of economic opportunity and a wish by staff not to become limited to an organization that either may not exist in the future or may not want to employ them then.

Market research feeds the knowledge base of an organization, whether it is a commercial one or one that is not for profit, and therefore feeds the essential asset of the organization; at its best it greatly contributes to its information climate. Because of the leakage of knowledge that is associated with staff turnover (voluntary or enforced), market research if anything will become more important in the future, not less.

The nature of the knowledge that best fits the operational process-driven requirements of most organizations is explicit knowledge, and as will be shown later in the book, this tends to favour the use of quantitative research (see Chapters 6 and 7). Quantitative information is also the type of information that fits most easily into the mechanical knowledge management systems that are spreading through large commercial organizations. Unfortunately, it is increasingly evident that the decisions that large organizations have to make are too complex to be reduced to simple mechanical models. This creates a tension in the way organizations are currently run and managed (and the temperament of the human resource that makes them up), as they seem to increasingly to need to draw on the softer, more conceptual type of tacit information. This can only be provided and conceived in terms of qualitative research ideas and an integrated approach to information interpretation, the management of which is still in the formative stages.

3 Decision making in an organization

Organizations are dynamic entities that are positively attempting to impact on the outside world. The decisions of a big organization are made in the millions every day by employees at all levels of the hierarchy. Most decisions are simply rule-bound or heuristic decisions, the rules of which are effectively integrated into the knowledge of the company; others are new decisions, generally because the rule does not exist (and these are often tactical in nature); still others, though rarer, are strategic decisions. The ease of decision making in an organization relates, in part, to its size, the level of politics that takes place and the coherency and comprehensiveness of the information climate. All may be influenced by the way the organization is structured. This chapter looks at the way companies go about making decisions and the role that market research has, or could have, in them.

KEY POINTS

- Organizations make most of their daily decisions by rote, using simple rules based on experience or common practice.

- Decisions relating to change require more thought, and may involve the *direct* use of market research.
- If a proper information climate exists in the organization, change decisions may be made based just on thought. In this case, the accumulated history of conducting market research in the company has an *indirect* influence.
- This indirect influence is rarely recognized, but can be more potent than a specially commissioned piece of work. This is because of the resultant decision being made on broader (and generally more assimilated) knowledge.
- The decisions that organizations make can look odd from the outside. This is generally because the external viewer is not in possession of all the information. Occasionally though, the decision is just odd.
- Decisions can be intimately involved in the power politics of an organization, and when this is the case, market research tends to be involved for better or worse.
- As organizations increase in size, it becomes more difficult for them to make the larger decisions due mainly to the multiplicity of internal cross-links that are needed and because of increasing remoteness from their customers. The organizational structure, and its relevance to today's decision making, then becomes a limiting factor.
- The problem becomes very large when dealing with international organizations with global brands and to counter this, it is necessary for these organizations to put management control systems into place, which try to balance central and local issues. There seems to be no set answer to this organizational problem, and organizations go through cyclical phases, swinging from one extreme to the other.

INTRODUCTION

This chapter looks at the way that decisions are made in organizations and the relationship that market research has to the process.

The factors impacting on the decision making ability of an organization are its size, the way it is organized, the comprehensiveness of its information climate, and the politics at the individual and cultural levels. All these factors are interrelated.

The size of an organization is important where the decisions are to be made at an organizational level; this generally means strategic decisions. The reason for this is that there are many cross-links that need to be taken into account and which can impede the flow of information. Normally, large organizations put into place structures to help with decision making at the company level, effectively to overcome the intrinsic inefficiency of being large (though naturally this also brings great benefits). Part of the skill of doing this is to have an organization that is not simply linear and hierarchical (which is very effective for handling day-to-day matters), but also has the means of crossing between sectors. Typically this involves locating staff functions at the head office.

Size and organizational factors influence how well the organization is aligned, and this translates down to the effectiveness of the information climate. It is very easy for different part of the organization to be thinking about the world in different ways, and this could include its markets and brands. If this is the case, strategic decision making becomes very hard, and conducting research for it becomes exceptionally so. This is because the research stakeholders will hold not just different perspectives, but different and incompatible assumptions too. Chapter 4 refers to different ways in which the market research function is organized in businesses.

However, apart from the difficulty of making decisions due to misunderstandings and problems with information flow, there are much more potent forces at play. These relate to the fact that personal futures are often entangled with decisions, and there can consequently be alternative agendas in place that are attempting to pervert the decisions to be made. All this is just a manifestation of human nature, but it is important because market research can be closely involved at these times, and furthermore this involvement is more likely if the decision is in any way 'difficult'.

Apart from the individual politics that everyone engages in from time to time, it is apparent that some organizations are more political than others. This is an aspect of their culture, and its presence is not necessarily good or bad. However, it is extremely important to keep an eye out for it and for market researchers to have an appreciation of what is going on.

This chapter seeks to open up these issues. It will first look at the normality of the majority of decisions a company makes, then examine the extra complexity that is introduced by the human factor – namely politics (which may be benign) – and finally it will look at organizational issues brought about by the size of the company, as manifest at its extreme in international companies.

THE PSYCHOLOGY OF DECISION MAKING

Being logical

The decision making process of a company is similar to the way that an individual goes about making decisions. In most cases it is obvious what to do: the individual has come across the situation many times before and over time, through experience, has worked out the best way of handling it; in effect, he or she has developed a set of rules about what to do. However, these rules are rarely written down (as there would be very many of them) and as such are tacit (in the original meaning of the term: see Chapter 2). That is, they could be written down if anyone could be bothered. Sometimes the rules, built up on the basis of experience within a company, are quite clear and categorical, but in many cases they are not. In this case the rules often interact, and effectively become a collection of principles. As such their application is often the subject of debate with oneself, or in the case of a company, others employed in it. A sort of 'playing' with the principles takes place until the outcome (the decision) 'feels' right. Management hierarchies have a legitimate role here, in being the arbiter of which principles take precedence in a particular case. This process would, of course, be very difficult to make explicit, and is an illustration of why the organic approach to knowledge management seems the one most likely to be successful in the future (see Chapter 2).

Sometimes, it does not seem to be possible to make a decision without some further information, and typically this is information of the factual type. This might be to clarify the nature of the problem (so as to know which rules to apply, or which principles to debate), to clarify the options available or simply to get the answer. Much information that is collected in this way is of quite an informal nature and may be general, very limited in scope and impressionistic. Often the information that is required is readily available, in a book for example, or on an Internet site or just by talking to someone. The amount of effort people put into this data collection task depends very much on the importance of getting the decision right, or more likely the consequences of getting it wrong. However, very rarely do people consider it worthwhile to commission bespoke research to get this information, which is why so many decisions are made without the help of market research.

Given all this, the person who has the task of making the decision may be unable to make one. The person may simply be incapable of it, he or she may feel uncomfortable about it because he or she perceives that he/she lacks some aspect of the process (information, for example, or senior management advice), or he/she simply does not want to make the decision at all – it may involve too much personal risk.

The human factor

The consequence of a decision is some form of a outcome: we make a decision so that we can do something and, as stated in Chapter 1, organizations are entities that 'do'. But the outcome that we come to may not be to everyone's taste, so that others may oppose it. They may oppose it because they think it is the wrong outcome, that it will cause damage in some way, or they may opposed it because of the political implications of it. It might be the right decision for the organization, but certainly not the right decision for a particular person. So a person may well want to stop someone else making a decision, and there are many ways in which he or she can make it difficult for that person to do so. It could be suggested that the nature of the problem has been misinterpreted, the information used to inform the decision making process has been faulty, the analysis of it is incorrect, the range of the possibilities kept too restricted or the significance of them misunderstood. There is no one so creative as one who wishes to pervert the course of a decision that he or she does not want made.

Actually, when a debate of this type takes place it may be based on perfectly legitimate reasons, not personal selfish ones. This occurs when the research has not been properly designed (or more rarely, not properly executed), and in particular has not taken into account the views of the various research stakeholders. When this happens, the normal course of events is to take a big breath and make the best of what one has, and try to smooth ruffled feathers. This is never a pleasant experience, which is why considerable effort should be put in to preventing it happening. Chapter 8 examines how to prevent this in some detail.

However, all this is nothing compared with the cases when the 'dark forces of power' are at work, and these can come from unexpected sources and directions. The aim is straightforward – to rubbish the research so that the decision that it implies should be made is thwarted. In the rubbishing of the research, there is also a quite explicit attempt to rubbish the researcher.

It is at times like this that the difficulty of the market research function comes to the fore (Hammond, 1998). Success in handling these issues, which does mean occasionally having a fight, makes the difference, for example, between the function degrading to a simple buying department with low status and poor prospects, or growing in status and influence and thereby being able to contribute potently to the success of the organization.

HANDLING CHANGE

It is convenient to think of change as either incremental or sudden. Sudden change is a shock, but in that it may affect one organization it is as likely to affect another, so bad as it may be, one is not alone in suffering. Incremental change, however, is much more pernicious and all the more so because it can easily go unnoticed. The bigger the organization, the more likely this is. It is also the case that organizations that have had a good historic success and found the 'winning formula' are more prone to this problem. The general feeling is 'Why fix it if it's not broke?'

In the short term, not adapting to small environmental changes has little impact on the performance of the organization (because the issues can be fudged), but in the end it becomes impossible to deny that all is not well. The problem now is that it can be virtually impossible to put the issues right as they are undoubtedly deep-rooted and going to require heavy investment (not easy for an ailing organization). Worse still is that a massive culture shift will be needed, which means loss of people. Unfortunately, no matter how carefully this is done (and generally, it is not done with any care at all!), the organization is always damaged by this and bleeds. At this point the organization has really to ask itself what right it has to exist at all – actually many organizations in this state do not continue to exist for long. This all argues for a constant questioning of the status quo, and market research is one way of doing this. Chapter 11 considers this in more detail.

THE ROLE OF MARKET RESEARCH

All of the above is trying to show that there are many dimensions to the way that an organization goes about making its decisions, and that market research is only a small part of this. However, it is still an important part, and this becomes more so as the organization gets bigger.

One of the largest problems that companies face is to get their personnel to think in an *aligned* way. Alignment can occur (or not!) across a whole series of different issues, and where market research can make a contribution is to get people to agree on the structure of the market, the motivations that are manifest in its dynamics and in the meaning of the brands that make it up. Furthermore, this common view should be constantly changing in synchronization with the market itself – which of course argues for there being constant engagement with the consumers and the market through the use of market research. The alternative is the growth of diverse cultural myths that can be used to argue anything, and can limit the ability of market research to contribute to the company.

Market research is deeply involved in feeding the internal knowledge of an organization, and is therefore a 'living activity' closely related to the functioning of organizations. It should not exist just as a set of projects in drawers, but within the mind of the people of the organization in terms of the *consequences* of having completed the research projects, manifest as a coherent view of all the different bits of information that are available. This means that the organization can make more sense of its information and that market research thereby contributes *indirectly* to its decision making, whether it is the daily little decisions that form the main life of the company, or the big decisions on which the very future of the company may rest.

When market research is working in this way, it is actually making its most powerful contribution. The reason is that the decision is being made as a result of the confidence the people have in the information climate of the company (see Chapter 2). It is not necessary to commission a new piece of market research either to know what to do, or as importantly, to convince other people. The people in the company are aligned with respect to their information and this produces immense efficiencies.

Furthermore, it can actually be better if new research is not commissioned, not for the obvious reasons that such research will cost money and take time, but because if the decision can be made in the information climate it is likely to be better and more balanced. The reason is that a new piece of market research can be disruptive – it will always produce new information that gives a 'new take' on all the old information. It will require a small shift in thinking to assimilate, and while this is good for the information climate in the long term, it is a bit distracting to the actual task in hand.

Because of the way that market research can influence the entire thinking of an organization, the decision an organization reaches after seeing the results of some research can sometimes, from an outside perspective, seem bizarre (Goodwin and Wright, 1997). This is entirely because the decision is based on more information than is delivered by the research.

However, this situation of a developed information climate is an ideal one that does not often happen: more often the situation is one in which the company has a series of cultural myths (see Chapter 2). These myths are very damaging as they adversely impact on the research design, which generally is quite tightly specified, and therefore reflects these incorrect hypotheses. Sometimes the specification can be so tight that the outcome is effectively ordained, and because of the constraints that are imposed upon the research by these cultural myths, it ends up incorrectly reinforcing them. There is some evidence that this is more of a problem than is generally recognized. For example, brand research often disregards important information about the sector (Cowan, 1994); only recently has an attempt been made to create a research product to address this (Callingham and Baker, 2001).

Putting this aside, organizations generally have to make decisions on the basis of a single research project, and for the research to impact on a decision a number of factors must be present (Smith and Fletcher, 1999). Clearly, the research has to meet the primary objective of the commissioner and associated stakeholders, so care has to be taken about getting this right. It is extremely easy to get this wrong (this will be explored in greater detail in Chapter 8). However, once this has been done, the output has to be manageable and the findings clear and memorable. They have to be realistic in that any actions suggested are achievable; they must be credible and believable and fit in with preconceptions, or at least it must be clear why they do not. These are all essential requirements for a piece of research to impact a decision.

However, it is always salutary to remember that market research does not in itself drive a company; it is the people in it that do this.

Market research is more like the oil of an engine enabling it to run smoothly and well. How well it does this depends on the way the company organizes itself, and to push the analogy a little further, no amount of oil will make a poorly designed engine anything else, while an absence of oil will mean even the best engine has only a short life.

THE INTERNATIONAL COMPANY

Just as large companies have bigger problems in managing themselves than small companies, especially in the areas of knowledge, the problems become even further intensified in multinational companies (Pawles, 1999). In fact, international companies have all the problems of smaller ones in the separate layers of their company, as well as the new problem of handling an organization spreading over many countries. So what are the aspects of international companies that are different, and what drives this?

As companies and markets have progressively become more international, the need to have global brands has grown in parallel. The reasons are economies of scale and the opportunities of global media. The key economy of scale is the cost of production, which is very high if the same brand is produced in many different versions in many different factories. Reducing the number of places in which a brand is produced can have a radical effect on profitability by making company assets work harder, thereby reducing the cost of working capital (see Chapter 2).

However, one of the characteristics of international companies is that they often have a very large brand portfolio because the company has collected brands as it has acquired companies in different countries. In many instances, it is not atypical for the top 10 per cent of brands to represent 90 per cent of turnover, and thus there is always pressure to rationalize brands and 'cut the tail' of the less profitable small, but global, brands. A major problem is how to rationalize the total set most effectively and achieve the economies of scale desired. *Brand portfolio management* is one of the biggest problems that a number of multinational companies are facing today.

The problem is that a brand may be doing well in one country, but have only a small share in another, so the questions are, what is its potential globally, and of all the contenders, which are the few that should be spread? Even worse is the issue of changing a brand that is small at the global level, but which provides the main source of profit for the national organization in its home territory.

Sitting in corporate HQ, the issue is quite simple: the larger the share that can be achieved from the fewer brands, the better the profit margins. But the world looks different from the local national perspective and as it is the people working in the national organizations who have to deliver national targets to corporate HQ, they have to be listened to. This is an example of the different perspectives of the research stakeholders referred to in Chapter 1, and it would not be surprising that the political dimensions referred to earlier in this chapter also come into play more than would be wished.

Market research is an important way in which this issue can be handled, but the complexities in it are as much human as technical.

Global brands

The nature of brands was described in Chapter 1: a brand name enables an item to be sold for more than its intrinsic value. Brands have a psychological aspect to their offer, and exist within a competitive framework. In fact the meaning of a brand only exists in people's heads, and this meaning is developed in part by reference to the universe in which they sit. The consequence of this is that while commodities do largely have similar meaning in different cultures (although this is not always the case), the question arises whether it makes any sense at all to talk about global brands. The product may be identical in form, packaging and advertising (although mostly this is not true either), but does it exist in people's heads in the same way from country to country?

In fact, brands do seem to translate across cultures, as often it is the very aspect of western culture that is part of what is being purchased. However, there are quite difficult problems in getting cross-country comparisons that are meaningful. This is for a number of reasons.

First, the nature of the people using a brand may sometimes be very different. In the developed western country, the brand may be almost a commodity, while in less developed countries, the brand may be used by only a small section of the population which is probably affluent and urban. The frequency of use may therefore be very different, and the brand may even be used in a different way or for a different purpose.

This will greatly influence the semiotics of using the brand although, as it turns out, it seems that the most powerful global brands tend to have very similar appeal in all markets.

Second, the market sector in which the brand falls (if it is the same) may be populated by a widely varying ranges of brands that collectively have quite different brand propositions from one country to another. The brand position may therefore be different as the brand is in a different context. Many product categories have very different histories even in closely neighbouring markets where different brands have been on the market. This has to be understood because it can lead to the need to emphasize different benefits in marketing communication.

Third, the meaning of colours, shapes and other iconic features of the brand may assume different cultural significance across countries and lead to further difficulties in interpretation. This can sometimes be unexpected and always needs to be checked before a brand is launched in a new market.

Fourth, markets can be in different state of 'western' evolution and also can occasionally go through sudden and dramatic changes as the political or economic environment changes. This can lead to rapid changes in market performance and the need for local management to react very fast.

All of this is further complicated by the fact that countries may additionally have strong sub-regional differences because of religious, ethnic or tribal factors in a way that it is difficult to understand from a western perspective. It is always essential in global marketing to have a good understanding of cultural differences across countries and regions that may influence the way that consumers in different countries decode brand communication.

Given these difficulties, one may question the value of creating global brands, and often the local operating companies of a multinational organization do exactly that. This leads to a tension building up between them and the centre, and market research can get involved right in the middle of this debate. This tension, if correctly handled, is a positive one if it leads to rational debate based on consumer understanding. On the other hand, if the debate ignores the evidence and is driven by emotion, it can lead to the dispersion of much energy. Successful companies have institutional mechanisms to control and channel this debate.

Management of global marketing

Multinational companies are presented with the problem of how best to organize themselves. Generally speaking the centre effectively controls the capital investment in each of its operating companies, while the operating companies have responsibility to achieve sales and profit targets. This is the basis of the power struggle, as each needs the other. Often, multinationals try to arrange themselves as regional groups, but it is mostly the case that some regions are compact and have high turnovers, while others are very geographically dispersed and have low turnovers. Some regions can therefore easily become 'more equal' than others, and this can mean they attract more of the capital and more of the influence on the brand development. For example, people from the more powerful countries are more likely to populate corporate HQ.

The marketing function is one of the many that has to be sensitive to the complexities of working in an international environment, and decisions have to be made about whether the function is organized centrally, regionally or locally, and whether this organization is deliberately in alignment with the operational organization, or structured to be in conflict with it.

One important role of a marketing department is to organize the advertising. The creation of campaigns that 'work' across countries is very difficult (but not as difficult as getting all the countries to buy into it!), because the most appropriate advertising vehicle may need to be different from country to country to deliver a common brand proposition. Powerful global brands such as Coke, Pampers, Lux, Dove, Close-Up and Head and Shoulders tend to alternate between three extremes. The first is the full global campaign such as Coke's 'Teach the world to sing' campaign. The second is to have a global advertising concept, which is executed in different ways, or using different vehicles in each region according to local consumer needs. An example of this was the Close-Up 'kissing' campaign – this is about young people who after using Close-Up get close up to each other – which ranged from an extremely raunchy kiss in Brazil to a very demure smile in India and China, although the underlying idea and brand positioning was the same in all countries (Pawles, 1999). The third way is to develop different campaigns in each region and country, but to a common advertising brief so that the advertising looks entirely different but the effect on brand image is similar.

It should never be forgotten that in the broad complexity of the world, the discipline of marketing is differentially developed. This means that the language used in different countries, although common across the world, has different conceptual meaning (Goodyear, 1996). This has important ramifications in designing the brief. For example, 'to market' could mean a television campaign in one country, or to literally 'take to the market' in a less sophisticated country.

Managing international market research

In all this, knowledge is power, and a question similarly arises as to whether the market research function should be run from the centre or from within the regions. A regional approach means that some regions simply cannot afford the cost of employing a specialist, while others can employ a whole team. A local approach means that the research is 'closer to the customer' and the particular features of the market can be easily taken into account, but the downside is that getting a global view at the centre becomes virtually impossible (Harrison and Ingledew, 1988).

One approach is to spread the responsibilities, doing work from the centre for decisions that have to be taken in a global context, and leaving research that is going to be used in a local context to be done locally. However, this does not stop local research ending up being presented to the centre, nor the 'inappropriateness' of the centre's research being pointed out to the centre when it seems 'necessary' to do so! Another approach is to have a central research function which lays down guidelines and gives advice on best practice. This means that research is collected according to common methods and therefore can be directly compared (in theory) even if very little of the research is commissioned from the centre.

The servicing of international companies is increasingly being done using international servicing groups, typically management consultant or accountancy groups. This is spreading to the marketing function, where the perceived need for global advertising is most easily achieved through using an international advertising group. Similarly, international research agencies or networks are increasingly doing the major research evaluation activities such as advertising tracking, and in response to this, global research agencies and networks are being formed and consolidated.

CONCLUSION

In Chapter 1, it was shown that organizations come in many different forms, and that this predicated the sort of research that they do. Organizations also come in very different sizes, ranging from a solo operative to huge global companies. This determines whether they do research at all and where their focus of interest is.

The decisions that a company makes will be informed by the information that the company has, which in turn is informed in part by market research. But decisions may not be wholly rational, and there may be political undercurrents working away. It should also be recognized that when a company makes a decision that appears to be stupid, it might actually be so, though in general it is rational.

All of this impacts greatly on the role of market research in a company and the difficulty of getting such research as is commissioned to be the right research.

4 The market research function within an organization

Market research departments have been the historical way by which the larger commercial enterprises have bought and managed their research. Although the death of the research department has been heralded for some time, it is still present in many companies although it may well be operating under another name. The traditional function of a research department was, in effect, to be the custodian of the company's information about brands and markets, and normally this was done from the perspective of the consumer. This would involve managing the information environment, teaching best practice to the company and its employees, acting as a central resource for buying the research and being available to help in its interpretation. In recent times there has been a growing dissatisfaction with the service provided by the research industry, and therefore with the research departments that lie within companies. This has translated into an increasingly stated need to have 'consumer insight', which seems to mean the ability to conceptualize the world from the consumer's point of view. It is probable that the source of this change is the greater knowledge that exists in the marketing community about research as a result of the very much greater volume of it being done, and the fact that it is now generally taught on undergraduate business courses. Clearly, in the long term this is a positive thing for the industry.

KEY POINTS

- Market research departments have always had a role greater than just buying market research.
- This role includes an educational one, a best practice one, and one relating to managing and harbouring the brands and market knowledge of the company.
- The organization of market research departments becomes difficult when the company is large, and there is a dilemma about whether to centralize or to distribute it. This is especially relevant to large international consumer companies.
- As the amount of market research experienced by a company and the marketing community increases, there has been an increasing amount of criticism about its ability to deliver better insight, and moves are afoot to create 'consumer insight' departments.
- This move reflects a fundamental shift in thinking about market research, in that such groups are effectively charged with removing the caveats that researchers generally put on their findings.

THE MARKET RESEARCH DEPARTMENT

This chapter is short, as it sets the scene for the way market research is managed in an organization and links strongly to the chapters that follow.

Many organizations have a group of people dedicated to providing information from survey research to the organization. In commercial companies this has historically been called the market research department, but is now increasingly being called a customer or consumer insight group, and this change in name does reflect a genuine difference in intent which will be explored later in the chapter. In this chapter the term 'market research department' will be taken to mean that group of people that are involved in buying and managing the output of survey research.

Basic function of the market research department

The function of a market research department varies from company to company, but in general it covers the following areas:

- To provide a point at which all the buying of research is made, so that there is one point in the organization that can manage this to reduce overlap and duplication.
- To provide a centre of expertise for the management of the purchasing of research (see Chapters 6 and 7).
- To manage the supplier-buyer interface (see Chapter 5).
- To ensure that the research purchased has a design appropriate for the job (see Chapter 8).
- To manage the research process from inception to results and further (see Chapters 9 and 10).
- To provide a point where help can be given over the interpretation and weight that should be put on research.
- To argue for good practice in the use of research.
- To help with the integration of different information sources to a common end.
- To act as a custodian of the marketing knowledge and history of the company's brands.
- To provide a single place where market research reports are kept, and where access to them is available to the whole organization.
- To help with the creation of an information climate for the company with respect to the markets in which it trades.

All these tasks seem innocuous enough, but as was mentioned in Chapter 3, market research gets intimately involved in the decision making process, which can involve power struggles within the organization. This means that at any moment it can find itself caught between powerful forces within the company, a position which can be extremely uncomfortable and very difficult to manage. However, success in this task is vital if the organization is to benefit from the value of market research. Later in this chapter, these issues will be developed.

Location in the organization

Not infrequently, the market research department is located within the marketing function and the research manager then reports to the marketing director or vice-president of marketing. Under these circumstances the department can be strongly influenced by what the marketing director thinks. However, quite often the department will have a life of its own, having been in existence for some time before the current marketing director joined. It is therefore possible that the department will have built its own ethos, which sets the standards of the way research is conducted within the company. The current marketing director then becomes the current custodian of the department.

However, the research department is sometimes organizationally detached from the marketing department, having a wider remit than simply serving requests from marketing. There are, after all, many company departments that can require market research other than the marketing department, such as human resources, operations, buying, internal communications and external affairs. Also, given the role that market research can have in evaluating marketing projects, some companies feel more comfortable if the resource is not directly under the control of the marketing function. However, such an arrangement tends to increase the detachment of the department from its internal clients (which can have its downside), but throws more responsibility on it to be the custodian of best practice.

Leadership function of the research department

A market research department can sometimes have a leadership role in the company with respect to the way the company grows its knowledge. This leadership dimension means that it is necessary for it to have an active educational role. In practice, it is rare that the research department has much actual power and it needs to use persuasion to discharge its responsibilities. Often it is the case that people in the research department have been in the company for a longer time than most of the people they do work for: staff movements tend to be more frequent among marketing people than market research people. Fortunately the greater authority that this endows researchers can actively help the process of maintaining standards within the community as a whole.

The educational role is basically teaching marketing people and others about the elements of market research, the ethical standards under which it operates, to have reasonable expectations of what it can do, and to generally feel comfortable with it. Fortunately, as the market research industry is well organized in the United Kingdom, essentially through the medium of the Market Research Society and other groups, there is a common set of views that internal researchers can pass on. Consequently, marketing people tend to meet them again and again as they change jobs, which naturally has the effect of reinforcing these ideas in their heads.

The importance of this educational role should not be underestimated as the cumulative effect of this is that many marketing people now have a very good understanding of market research and are able to use it in a sensitive and sensible way.

Organizational changes are afoot

As was observed earlier in the chapter, organizational separation and concentration of expertise into a large research department can have its downside. This is because the gap between the end-user and the internal supplier becomes too great and there is a loss of mutual understanding. In these circumstances, the internal research department might just as well be outside the buying organizations and its value becomes degraded.

This problem can be addressed by splitting up the department into smaller and more focused business groups. Very large organizations (especially international consumer companies) have found this to be a better way of handling their research for a number of years now, because each of the business groups has its own experience and expertise. The individual departments can, therefore, better see the picture from their point of view, and better make a contribution to consumer insight.

The end result of this process, which is happening in a number of cases now for the first time, is to fragment the research department entirely and to build its personnel into the individual brand groups as their own information specialists, generally called 'planner', 'consumer insight manager' or some such title.

Whether to concentrate researchers together or to disperse them entirely through the end-user groups is ultimately to trade off benefits, and doubtlessly it will be a pendulum that swings this way and that. Concentration has advantages associated with expertise, longevity of information, breadth of market perspective and the educational role, while fragmentation has the advantage of intensification of knowledge locally, which is largely where the decisions are made.

CONSUMER INSIGHT

Putting aside the organizational changes that are taking place, there is also a fundamental change with respect to the expectation of the outcome of market research. These changes are putting much greater weight on the broader-based understanding of markets and brands, and do not sit happily with the more cautious approach that market researchers typically display. Typically, debates are moving to being about the differences between 'data', 'knowledge' and 'wisdom' and how one can move from one to the other. Such debates have been around for a number of years, but their intensity has become greater recently. This is because a criticism that is now levelled at market research is that it is 'only' data and what is now wanted is 'consumer insight'; internal functions are now being set up to deliver it. There is very little written about what 'consumer insight' is, though there seems to be little doubt that it is urgently wanted and in copious amounts too! (Coates, 1998).

Historically, the *market analysis* function has not been located within the market research department. This is because the information used has been quite different from that used in market research and has required different types of skill. In fact, the orientation in approaching market analysis is philosophically very different from market research in that the data that is to be analyzed is already available and 'ordained' in its structure while market researchers typically design the data set to help with solving a problem. It is also the case that the 'clients' for the output of market analysis have typically been salespeople rather than marketing people, and that the orientation of these two groups is different.

As will be discussed in Chapter 7, there is real difficulty in extracting information from the various sales and market information sources that the company has access to, and the results of this apparently objective process are always ultimately ambiguous. The reason is the multiplicity of ways that the data can be analysed for the different functions within the company. This includes the complexity of identifying which factors that were supposed to influence the market have actually done so, and untangling these effects from exterior influences on the market that might be quite unexpected – but more on this later.

The net effect is that it is increasingly being recognized that the output requirements of market research and market analysis have been moving together, and some of the new insight departments are actively trying to combine the 'insight' of both.

'Consumer insight' is a manufacturer's term. The same processes causing its creation have already happened in advertising agencies, where the term 'planner' has been used for many years (Shaw and Edwards, 2000). The experience in advertising agencies is that many have moved away from accepting the role that properly constituted research can play, and it seems almost culturally acceptable to say that quantitative research is boring, incomprehensible, and therefore should be discarded. This is a regrettable trend, as clearly, anything that can help in getting better decisions should be used, but researchers have only themselves to blame for this trend as they have not conveyed the benefits well (see Chapter 6).

It is possible that a similar change could occur within the commissioning environment in the future, and this would really be a step backwards. It is most likely to occur in those environments that have fragmented their research resource across the brand groups. In such cases it must be very difficult to control conventional research standards, and to ensure some form of continuity of good practice.

An obvious route forward would be to have both researchers and insight managers working alongside one another. The researcher role could then be to ensure that the data was collected in a reasonable way, and, in such an environment, researchers could actually be liberated to be even more tedious and to argue caution in the interpretation of the results. The insight managers would then have a firm base on which to develop their more broadly based 'market and brand insight', sure in the knowledge that they had not been 'taken over' by their enthusiasm about a possible outcome. This is not to say that one person could not do both roles; only that it would be extremely difficult to do both roles simultaneously.

Although it is easy to see the term 'consumer insight' as simply a relabelling, it nevertheless reflects a change of importance. This is increasingly arising due to the greater familiarity the end-user clients have with market research (many have undertaken courses on market research at university) and the huge amounts of it that are around in companies. This has produced a less reverent feeling towards the whole subject, and a greater level of impatience with researchers who go on and on about the caveats.

The critical change that seems to be happening is of moving from individual data sources to the synthesis of something greater from the constituent parts, and also the inclusion of common knowledge (and sense!) in the process. Chapter 11 describes some of the groundbreaking approaches that are emerging around us to achieve a full synthesis of the type required, but with some form of rigour and without the tedious limitations that market research has traditionally suffered.

THE POWER THING AGAIN

The nature of people who go into information specialist roles is really quite distinct in that they tend to be curious and naturally investigative: on the whole they are not combative. Many people in the operations part of the company (which tends to be the majority of the company these days) have a clear task to do – to make something happen – and as has been mentioned before, companies are 'doing' entities. Furthermore, success comes from doing things, often in the form of a bonus, and failure may mean the sack. Assertiveness, and the propensity to engage in battles, are therefore positive personality aspects for people in this role.

Given the concept developed in Chapter 1 of the research stakeholder, there are generally a number of different people interested in the outcome of a piece of research. For example, an advertising agency may be proposing a particular creative vehicle for a forthcoming campaign, and unknown to anyone in the client company, this idea is particularly cherished by the proprietor of the agency. The account executive therefore knows that it is in his or her best interests to persuade the client company of the merits of this particular approach. He or she will therefore get very twitchy if the client proposes some research into it (and why might the client want this anyway unless the client is not feeling comfortable with the approach?). The account executive will see the storm clouds ahead, and will want very much to be involved with whoever is going to do the research. He or she will want someone he/she knows, someone who is 'sensitive to advertising', someone who will not come down on an 'executional' detail but be able to see the 'strategy' behind the advert and therefore help to develop it. He or she will want to sit in on focus groups, and to know the outcome of the research before it is debriefed. If the account executive feels the research is 'going the wrong way', he or she will arrive late for the debrief, and ask aggressive questions throughout it: focusing on the structure of the sample, for example, and questioning the ability of the respondents to be aware of the meaning of the advertising anyway. The account executive will colour his or her comments in terms of what he or she personally saw happening in the groups (or at least his or her opinion about what was happening). He or she is likely to question the significance of the stimulus material used, and the experience of the researcher (who the account executive may privately express 'doubts' about, even though he or she was involved in selecting the researcher). Of course he or she will be very inventive about the particular model of advertising with which to question the findings, and so on.

There is no intention of singling out advertising research in this example, as this scenario can be present with any research. In fact one of the most important aspects to find out when settling the research brief is the possibility that there may be such undercurrents. Experience shows that these can develop apparently out of the blue, just when they are most damaging.

The research department can react in one of two ways to this situation: it can cave in and agree to all this nonsense (although sometimes it is true – and that's a difficulty), or try to fight it. But in a war one always needs allies, and these are developed before the event, not during it. The strongest ally of all is a reputation for integrity, and that the research department's opinion matters very much precisely because it has no axe to grind on the findings other than that they should be true. This characteristic of a research department is not ordained, it has to be won, and achieving it is a gradual process involving winning people over as they join the company and having their support as they get promoted through it.

One aspect of changes in company organizations is to adopt an internal customer service approach: that is, that everyone is a customer of someone else. This is a device to remove the bureaucracy from organizational hierarchies, and has a lot of merit to it. However, what also comes with this is a series of 'bosses' who have no responsibility – they can be very demanding customers and stamp their feet accordingly. Living in a world where one is balancing the interest of different research stakeholders with the truth (when all the stakeholders think of themselves as customers) is not easy.

CONCLUSION

Market research departments have been found to be useful when a company is buying large amounts of market research, because they ensure that the money is well spent and that the use of the information already bought is maximized. In addition they can help to give confidence in the research at the point of decision. There are changes taking place in the organization of research, and typically this is now taking the form of an insight group. In other circumstances, the people involved have been distributed directly into the brand teams. Although these changes mean that information is more likely to be produced that is stripped of the caveats of the research world (which the end-user can find very tedious), and is therefore easier to appreciate and conceptualize, the experience of the introduction planners in advertising agencies (who seem to be the equivalent of insight managers), has shown that, over the longer term, the technical competence of appreciating the significance of the findings can be lost. The industry is therefore at a turning point in the organization of research within companies.

5 Buyer–supplier relationships

The buyers of research can be buying for themselves or for another internal end-user. In this latter case they will often be located in a market research department, and this can be a helpful or unhelpful intermediary. The research department mediates between the end-users and the industry, as it made up by the set of potential suppliers. It should know what is available in this market (really the various types of 'products' on the one hand, and the people on the other) and ensure that the selection of the agency or researcher is the most appropriate for the job. It should then make the life of the agency as easy as it can, so that it can put its mind to doing the work.

KEY POINTS

- Buying may be done directly by the end-user or by an entity in the organization on behalf of the end-user. The latter is more common in large organizations, both public and private.
- In the former case, where the end-user is also the commissioner of the research, the relationship between the buyer and the supplier may well be quite intimate, with the supplier acting as a confidant and a consultant. It is often the case that such a relationship exists between a supplier who is essentially a qualitative researcher, but who will handle such quantitative research as is needed as well.

- In the case where there is an internal buying organization, the buying entity will need to have a list of potential suppliers with which to match projects for particular internal clients. This becomes more important the bigger the organization that the buying entity serves.
- In the case of quantitative research, the list may be informal and comprise a series of agencies that offer specialist products. This list tends to grow as the research buyer gets more experience, and is fed by conference papers, agency pitches, adverts and the like. It tends to be price driven for standard work, technique driven for more specialized work and occasionally driven by the ability of the agency to offer imaginative original research designs.
- Factors that affect the choice of a qualitative supplier are much more 'human' in nature, such as personality, temperament, research style inclination, market experience, as well as a number of simple logistic factors, such as availability.
- Creating and maintaining the qualitative researcher list, even if it is one of varying degrees of informality, is one of the harder things that an internal research buyer has to do. However, a very common way for a qualitative researcher to get on the list of an organization is through personal introductions and referrals.
- For reasons of speed and efficiency, most jobs in commercial organizations are placed without any form of competitive pitch, but in some cases a competitive pitch is required. This may be because there is uncertainty about the research method, a need to assess experience, or simply to try to be fair. The brief provided for the pitch may be very comprehensive or limited, and may require an initial briefing meeting. This can involve a lot of work on behalf of the pitching agencies (and for that matter the buying group), and this process needs to be handled with care to be fair and efficient to all parties. Ideally, those who are asked to pitch should know the number of others that have also been asked, and given some idea what they are particularly expected to bring to the party. Again ideally, those who have failed to win the pitch should be given some idea why this was so.
- Around every job there is an implicit contract as to what is expected. Generally the details of this are not spelled out and can cause problems if the job is perceived not to have worked well. Purchasing departments have the advantage in getting contracts that attempt to get these things written down.

- It is very important that the supplier is easily contactable, that he or she signals the presence of potential problems in the fieldwork, and prepares the client as to the nature of the results before the debrief. Similarly, it is important that the buyer is available, but also that he or she leaves the researcher alone to get on with the research.
- It is good practice for a post-research review to take place between the buyer and the supplier, though this is a rarity.

TYPES OF BUYING

It is convenient to separate the situation where commissioners of research are the end-user themselves from that where there is an internal research buyer (commonly the market research function within the company) who is buying on behalf of a number of internal end-using clients. This latter situation is worth further dividing into the occasions when the internal function has little status (or apparent use) from one where it does. In addition, there is the further complication of when a purchasing department is involved, which is often the case in many larger commercial organizations and in many government departments as well.

End-user buying

If the end-user clients are doing the commissioning themselves, they tend to build a close relationship with one supplier and put all their business through that supplier. The relationship that grows up is one of trust which is unlikely to break, as a sort of marriage bond has been formed and the external researcher is used as much as a confidant, whose opinion is respected, as a supplier of original data. Such a commissioner generally works with one preferred supplier because he or she does not have enough work to build up the level of experience required to get to know more suppliers.

This situation is often a very happy one. The reason is that the buyer/end-user can get help easily, and the likelihood is that it will be well thought out and considered help that gets better as the relationship grows stronger. One of the characteristics of this type of relationship (although this is not true in every case) is that the researcher tends to be of a qualitative orientation. This of course helps when it comes to providing an overall picture in which data is synthesized and integrated, but it can lead to the work being heavily biased towards being qualitative when perhaps more should have been quantitative. The advice given will also inevitably become more coloured by the particular experience of the researcher and may, therefore, unavoidably become narrow.

The internal research function does the buying

Organizations vary greatly in the way that they accommodate research. Some simply see no value in it at all, and consequently people are not encouraged to do it – and may be actively discouraged. Actually, research maybe of little value to an organization such as, for example, those organization that have some form of monopoly or are selling commodities or 'est' brands (see Chapter 1). Other organizations see research as facilitating tactical decision making, and are happy that it is done even though it may be conducted in a piecemeal way. This can be true of some large marketing companies. However, most of the larger users of research have found that it is better to coordinate it through some form of central resource, as the buying is performed more expertly and the results can be better coordinated and shared. Generally this is done through the medium of a market research or consumer insight department. Obviously, the function of a market research department should be much more than providing a point where expert buying of research takes place, and this was explored in more detail in Chapter 4.

In general, the presence of a market research department is welcomed by suppliers as it provides a point of expertise to which they can relate, and it generally understands the imperatives under which external researchers work. In this way it can smooth the passage of the whole process, and contribute to the ultimate work being used successfully in the organization (see Chapter 8).

However, many researchers also say that if the research function is weak, and only provides a buying function, it can positively damage the whole process. This seems to occur when the organization is essentially overtly political, and the power of the research function has been degraded within the organization. Such is human nature that the political dimension that provides the context to the research department internally extends to the relationship between it and its external suppliers, not in a helpful way but in a distinctly unhelpful way. Power politics become evident, and the external researcher is given edited information, and not allowed access to the end-user if he or she feels it is needed (which it often is in this situation). This corrupt relationship reduces the chance of the research being designed and executed effectively, and of the ultimate outcome being positive. Furthermore, at the debrief (see Chapter 9), the internal researcher 'sits on the end-user side' of the table and distances him- or herself from the researchers in order not to be associated with possible politically unacceptable results. Furthermore, should such unacceptable results appear, the internal researcher may well 'help' the end-user by criticizing the researcher on methodological grounds in order to 'invalidate' the findings.

Clearly, the role of research in such an organization is not about finding the truth, and it is likely that the organization (meaning the research department, and probably, in the end, the organization itself) will end up destroying itself.

PROPOSING AGAINST A WRITTEN BRIEF

Often, business is placed by a buyer with a researcher who he or she feels will be appropriate. This is an efficient method for both sides. However, in some cases agencies are asked to submit a proposal against a brief, and then a few of them will be asked to come and present their proposals. This is a long and time-consuming activity for the company, and will tend only to be undergone when the project is especially large or especially important to the people in the company. Government organizations are more likely to follow a process like this, as it appears to be fairer to the suppliers, and everything is more accountable. The agencies selected to be invited to tender will, on the whole, be 'on the list', but occasionally a new agency will be asked as well. This is an opportunity for the company to see the agency acting against a real project, and for the agency to show its credentials in a practical situation.

However, only one of the agencies will win the pitch, and all will have spent many hours producing their proposals, as well as the time spent presenting it if selected, so this seemingly 'fair' process may be anything but. It is therefore sensible for the commissioning company to limit as much as possible the numbers of agencies it involves, and tell them how many competitors they have. Obviously the commissioning company should know why it is asking the agencies to pitch, and it is helpful for the agencies to be told this reason, as it helps them to better orientate their proposal. It is also very helpful for the agency to have some indication of the price parameters.

In some cases the commissioning company may have a very good idea who is likely to win the pitch in advance, and may be going out to tender to check it is right. Under these circumstances the number of competing agencies should be very small. Alternatively, the company should be upfront about it and offer to pay for the time the research agencies are spending on creating the proposal.

It is a common misunderstanding that research buyers only select on price. This may in practice be true, but it will often be because the buyer can see no other way to differentiate between the proposals. It is an excellent thing for the commissioning company to give the criteria by which it intends to select the successful candidate. This is not very common, either because it is not thought to be included in the brief, or it is not thought about at all! The criteria for success can be quite different from one job to another, and from one commissioning company to another. It may be to do with pragmatic issues such as cost or timing, or it might be originality of design, the relevance of the experience claimed, the ability to match to previous work or any number of different things.

After the process is completed, the commissioning group has a lot of proposals which contain a variety of ideas. These ideas are the intellectual property of the submitting agencies (unless the proposal has been paid for) and should be treated as such – see the Market Research Society's Code of Conduct.

Whatever the basis for the final selection, it is good practice for the commissioner to go back to the non-winners to discuss their pitch and to explain why another was selected. Apart from being polite, it is also to the commissioner's advantage as it will help the agency submit more appropriate proposals in the future.

COMMISSIONING QUANTITATIVE RESEARCH

The nature of qualitative and quantitative information is quite different, and this will be explored in Chapters 6 and 7. The differences translate into the ways that it is commissioned, which tend to be more obviously rational and logical for quantitative data than for qualitative research, although as will be shown later in this chapter, the same amount of thinking goes into both cases.

Quantitative research can fall into two broad types: one involves comparatively simple quantification and the other uses special techniques or methods of analysis.

The work that is about simple quantification is really commodity based and therefore goes to the lowest cost provider. However, a number of issues arise here. First, it is apparent that the basic fieldwork should be done properly and in accordance with the standards the Market Research Society advocates, including conformance to the relevant elements of its Code. Ideally, the field force should also be a member of a recognized quality standards system such as the Interviewer Quality Control Scheme (IQCS) that operates in the United Kingdom. This all costs money and makes the job more expensive than it would be otherwise, so it is temping to go to providers that do not have these standards but do have a field force that can double up as market research interviewers. Placing business in this way is rarely sensible, because not only may the fieldwork not be carried out in accordance with the instructions, but also, without proper controls being in place to manage it, the data may end up being wholly invented. Furthermore, the quality of the responses is bound to be worse than those obtained by using properly trained interviewers.

There is also another reason for using a proper research agency on such work. This is because all jobs do need some design: that is, the sample, location, question set and tabulation specification all need to be decided upon. In addition, such quantitative jobs may not be as simple as they appear, and the design may require more than basic market research knowledge, and need thinking through properly and with originality (see Chapter 8).

However, the fact is that much can come out of simple quantitative research and that within the limits of the basic rudiments, this is normally bought from the lowest cost provider, or for some other sub-commodity 'est' reason (see Chapter 1).

In some cases, quantitative research can be used to support major decisions in a company, and even though the research may be quite simple, the choice of supplier then becomes important and political. In addition, in these cases the cost of it can be very high, which further adds to the sensitivity of the choice of supplier. In these cases, selection is done on the basis of reputation and specialization. For example, the selection of a advertising tracking agency is important because the contract will have to run for at least two years, and will therefore involve a lot of expense. Furthermore, it will be used to make decisions about the company's advertising, which generally involves a lot of money, but also is about the future of the brands that the company owns, which normally are worth even more. The research stakeholders in this case are necessarily important and varied. They will include the marketing function, the advertising agency or agencies and probably the board as a whole, as it has to support the continued investment in marketing. So the selection of the research provider in this case is complicated and important. Similar issues may surround other big tracking studies such as customer satisfaction.

Other types of use of a quantitative agency are when some specialized work is required such as pricing work, or brand positioning work. These tend to come up only occasionally, and the market of suppliers in each of these types of area is wide and the differences in their offerings generally not transparent. This is because there is often some form of proprietary element to the methodology that the supplier company wants to keep secret. A research buyer needs to invest a lot of work in order to keep on top of these specialist research suppliers and understand the nature of their offerings, as when the time comes for the company to do research in one of these areas, there will not be the time to catch up on one's homework.

At a more pedestrian level, it is important for a research buyer to know such things as the merits of the competing omnibus products that are available and where their strengths are. This could be simple things like the base size, the times that they run, the regions that they run in and the speed of turnaround.

The essential background information for a research buyer when buying quantitative work is a general knowledge of the research market industry and the products within it. To this extent, it is not very personality driven, which, as has already been mentioned and will be developed further, is the case in qualitative research buying. However, having said all this, it is always better when the research buyer has previously met someone in the agency that he or she is proposing to place business with, and this is the reason research pitches are better than straightforward adverts for quantitative research, and why building up networks through the conference circuit is important also.

IMPORTANT FACTORS WHEN COMMISSIONING QUALITATIVE RESEARCH

Commissioning qualitative research is either one of the easiest things a research manager has to do or one of the hardest, and consequently this section will be longer than the equivalent one for quantitative research.

If the commissioner is buying for internal end-user clients, he or she will, by necessity, have a list of preferred suppliers from which to choose for any particular job. The market research function has the task of maintaining a list of qualitative researchers of sufficient length for it to be able to manage whatever type and amount of work it has within the time limits that are required of it. As will be described later in this chapter, there are a number of criteria that apply to selecting a qualitative researcher for a particular job, and therefore it is essential to have some form of list of researchers of different types. The following are a series of aspects where qualitative research differs from quantitative research in ways that lead to a difference in the method of placing the business.

The importance of the personal 'connection'

Qualitative research findings are generally communicated at the debrief, where the researcher who did the work (or most of it anyway) is in front of the end-user client who generally needs to act on what he or she hears. This is very different from the situation that prevails in the case of quantitative research, where the researcher is presenting the findings of a survey expressed in numerical terms. In the qualitative researcher case, the presentation is about what conclusions the researcher has come to, through what can seem a mysterious process. It can all feel horribly subjective to the positive thinking businessperson who feels he or she may need to justify everything. The end-user has to trust in and believe the researcher in order for him or her to be able to have the confidence to make the necessary decisions. This is particularly the case when the decisions are counter to the expectations. Consequently, the personal chemistry between a researcher and the end-user is of vital importance and tends to colour choice very strongly.

Buyers of research are therefore always on the lookout for suppliers who 'fit' their organization. If the commissioner is a research manager commissioning on behalf of a variety of internal clients, he or she will additionally need to have a range of researchers available to match to the various internal personalities he or she is serving.

The need to match the qualitative researcher to the job

Even when one has achieved the hoped for good match of personality between the researcher and the end-user client, there are still a number of other factors to take into account. This is because qualitative researchers differ in the type of job they are best at, and this could be for a number of reasons.

Market familiarity

The knowledge that a qualitative researcher has of a particular market is sometimes considered to be very important. Sometimes it is genuinely the case that the market is complicated and difficult to come to grips with, although this should be possible to handle with a quality briefing. However, it is often useful for a researcher to have some familiarity with the market in order to handle offbeat questions in the debrief.

Sometimes the very fact that a researcher has knowledge of a market can be a problem, in that this knowledge may have been obtained by working with a competitor. Some end-users are very sensitive about working with researchers who do work for the competition. At a rational level, much depends upon when the competitor work was done and what degree of closeness was achieved between the competitor and the researcher – but many decisions are not rational. Some companies do not mind their researchers working for their competitors, either because they do not see the work as being of particular sensitivity, or because they are respectful of the researcher's integrity, or both. The decision is a two-edged sword, as many researchers do not want to work for companies that are in competition with one another.

Researchers have preferences for particular categories of research

Qualitative researchers differ in their affinity to various general categories of research (for example, new product development, advertising research, children's research). This may be to do with the nature of the techniques that work best (with which the researcher may or may not feel comfortable), or the people with whom the researcher needs to mix (not everyone, for example, likes working with advertising agencies), or the general output of the research required (for example, tightly defined and argued versus creative and more speculative).

Some researchers simply do not want to do certain types of research by virtue of the locations the researcher might be required to go. In-pub interviewing, for example, may not always be the most pleasant thing for women, as male respondents could well start flirting with them and not take them seriously, although again this is very dependent upon the type of pub one is talking about. Men can also feel uncomfortable doing in-pub work.

Demographics interaction

The demographics of the researcher may be relevant, as the similarity or differences of age and sex of the researcher and the respondents can influence the nature of the interactions that take place.

Variable workloads

An organization's need for qualitative research varies greatly, depending upon the projects running at any one time (and their stage). It could be that a number of projects require research at one time, while at other times it is comparatively quiet. Furthermore, research is often commissioned at very short notice for a variety of marketing, cultural and competence reasons. It is therefore not sensible for a commissioner of research to expect that a particular researcher will always be available to do a job within the timings required, because he or she is either already handling another aspect of the company's work, or working for someone else.

The resources of the supplying company

Some research projects are better handled by a single supplying person (or at least perceived as such by the client), while others need more than one person on the job for reasons of speed, scale or complexity. Some researchers prefer to work with another, as they feel the interaction enhances the quality of the output; others are less happy to do so as they feel they are not so tightly in control of what is happening.

Researchers have phases in their lives too

Researchers may become unavailable because they are going through a particular phase (they are human after all). They may decide that they are not going to supply research and take a break, for example to have children or to go round the world.

Normally, once a researcher has started on a project, any further work on the project will tend to be placed with that person. This is because the briefing gets easier and more efficient, and as important, there is also the chance (and generally the expectation) that the total knowledge on the project will compound.

The question whether to keep a single researcher on one project

The use of a single researcher on an ongoing project does have the disadvantage that other researchers do not get a 'look-in', and may feel that the company has rejected them as they may not be used for some time. However, it does happen occasionally, that the original researcher is not available for one stage of the project, so a new one is brought in and effectively inherits the project.

There are some who feel that the process of keeping a single researcher on one project is too restricting for the project, and puts too much emphasis on the opinions of one researcher. In practice, a researcher tends to stay on the project because it is easier for everyone if he or she does so.

CREATING THE QUALITATIVE LIST

For all the above reasons, internal buyers of research have to have a list of qualitative researchers with which they place, or whom they invite to tender for, business. As has been mentioned, this is one of the more difficult tasks for internal buyers of research.

At face value, this should be an easy task, as in fact there are very many very good qualitative market researchers around, and virtually no bad ones. Qualitative market research is a business in which one's reputation is extremely dependent on the last work done, and consequently, it is virtually impossible to survive unless one is consistently good.

A popular way of growing a list in a company is to ask newcomers to the company who they would like to use. It is therefore possible to use the newly recommended researcher on a job for their recommender, with a general expectation that the end-user will be satisfied – as it was his or her recommendation. It also means that the 'new' researcher can get exposure to the company, and a general judgement about the all-important personality issues can be made.

Another method is to have formal pitches to a group of people by a researcher, and a consensus agreement made whether to use him or her or not.

On the whole, adverts and directories do not help a qualitative researcher get on the list (whereas they are a help to quantitative agencies), although they do serve to maintain awareness and provide contact details, and of course to reawaken the idea of using a person who has not been used for some time.

Company pitches are quite common, but it is very difficult for one qualitative researcher to present him- or herself in a way that is distinct from another. The market appears quite generic, and as has already been said many times, so much depends on personality matching.

A researcher may, for some other reason, become unattractive to the commissioner through, for example, his or her skill base not matching the changing needs of the company, his or her personality not fitting the new internal client base, or through his or her being perceived (rightly or wrongly) to be no longer 'good'.

KEEPING THE CLIENT HAPPY

In market research, the researcher or agency is only as good as the last job. This is undoubtedly unfair, but unfortunately true. Most researchers do good jobs within the constraints that are imposed upon them, but still researchers get dropped from lists either by being deliberately axed, or simply by not getting any more jobs. An obvious reason for this is that the researcher is perceived to have done a 'bad job'. Occasionally, a research project may go wrong for all sorts of reasons, which could involve failure of the client, failure in recruitment, or just bad luck. However, another is that the researcher may have been 'off form' – ill, bored, uninterested, having personal problems, and so forth (see Chapter 10). Whatever the reason, it is quite likely that the researcher will get the blame, rightly or wrongly. Given the high stakes that can surround the outcome of research, long-term relationships can terminate quite easily if the conditions are right (or wrong!). This is all the more unfortunate as no researcher willingly makes this happen, and in general the problems are ones of misunderstanding, not ignorance or incompetence.

However, there are also a number of straightforward things that can upset a research buyer. Clients do vary greatly in what they expect and how they define a 'quality' job, and it is prudent to have an eye to their basic expectations, as this is essential to maintaining the relationship. The following sections describe the critical aspects of managing the relationship between the researcher and the client during the course of a job, which may influence the future relationship.

Contact

The ability for a researcher to be contactable is critical. Although researchers are often away from their desk, as is required by the nature of their work, clients expect to be able to contact them easily. Not only is good contact taken as a sign of a dedication of the researcher to the job, it is also a way in which any problem the buyer might have can be resolved. Failure to respond to contacts is really the death knell of a relationship, and with modern technology there is no reason good contact should not be maintained.

The buyer may wish to make contact in order to place the initial brief (which will probably have tight deadlines, and he or she will need to know whether the supplier is able and willing to take the job on), for organizing elements of the research process, for example, the stimulus material or contact details, for changes to the brief and so on.

Contact is a mutual thing and it is vital that the research buyer is also easily contactable. Unfortunately, the buyer does not always take the same view with respect to contact the other way, and this can be difficult.

Implicit aspects of the contract

A lot of research is placed with little in the way of documentation about the job itself, although there will be some form of brief created. However, even in a well-documented briefing there is much about the job that is unstated and implicit because it is seen to be obvious. This is the area where major problems can occur, because what is obvious to one person is not to another.

In qualitative research, the areas that need attention include: the number of people in a group, how many can have been in groups before, what happens if there has been a mis-recruitment, what is expected of client observers at the group, expectations of who is doing the moderation, use of transcripts in analysis, expectations of reporting and so forth.

In quantitative research areas requiring attention include matters of timing (it is important that a pre-advertising research wave takes place before the advertising starts!), the total base size being what was requested, the stimulus material not getting mixed up and so forth.

It is extremely tedious to tie all these things down, especially with the speed of job placement, and this is even worse when the time imperatives require a trade-off to be made against these 'normal' requirements with little guidance as to which the buyer might consider to be inviolate. Neither the buyer nor the supplier is especially interested in this until something goes wrong – when the 'proverbial' hits the fan.

Other issues that are really bad news are: taking the client for granted, acting in an insensitive way in the debrief, being late with documentation (especially reports if these were requested), spelling brand names incorrectly and generally letting the client down in a variety of unspecified ways.

This is where the role of a purchasing department can be helpful (if present), in that it has the expertise (and interest) to get a lot of this stuff into the basic contract that underwrites the researcher being on the roster.

Informing on progress

As mentioned earlier there is an essential difference between an end-user who is commissioning for him- or herself, and one who is commissioning on behalf of another. In the former case, the buyer will be keen to know of the results as soon as anything is available or half available. Managing this is a job that the researcher has to develop and be happy with, as it is not helpful to the analytical process to be asked constantly what the findings are.

In the latter case, the buyer will be busy with other activities and will not be particularly interested in the progress of any particular project, only that the job is progressing smoothly and according to plan. This is because the buyer will mostly not have a stake in the actual findings, only that the research was professionally conducted and worked well. Also, because the buyer will be working with researchers with whom he or she is familiar, he or she will presume that everything is going well, and not need reassurance of this. However, it takes little effort to email that the key stages have been successful, for example, and that the fieldwork has been completed successfully.

Managing the results

Although it is always good practice for a researcher (especially a qualitative researcher) to be left alone by the client while he or she is formulating the results (see Chapter 9), it is generally of value for him or her to give some idea about the outcome of the research before the formal debrief.

As has been mentioned, the research function in an organization will primarily be concerned that the research process has happened in a satisfactory way – and should know this anyway by the time of the debrief. However, by this time the department will also want to be able to prepare the way for managing the impact of the results on the end-user client, and will normally want some idea about the nature of the findings. In particular, it needs to have a feel for any information that might be controversial, both to help the researcher in how to handle it – and to prepare him or her for the sorts of questioning that might be coming – and to 'soften up' the end-user so he or she is not 'thrown' in the actual debrief – which is not helpful to anyone. Even bland sorts of information, such as 'There are no surprises', or 'It's good news', or 'It's bad news' really do help the debrief group to orientate itself before the debrief.

There are some buyers who actually like to spend the time with the researcher to influence the tone of the final presentation and to help with any potential political issues. This is not anything like as common for qualitative research as for quantitative.

Lunches

Given that personal relationships are important in this business, it is not surprising that an amount of entertainment goes on between supplier and buyer. Obviously there are a number of ethical considerations to take into account: for example, it is not normal to take a person out to lunch before work has been commissioned as this could be construed inappropriately. Many researchers do not take clients out to lunch at all and manage their businesses perfectly well, while others are much more inclined to do so. Some clients relish being taken out, others avoid it, and some organizations, especially in the public service domain, actively discourage it.

Feedback

It is always good practice for the commissioning client to give some sort of feedback to the researcher after the debrief. This is rarely done enough. The reason is that generally the work is delivered to expectation, and therefore there does not seem to be much to say. When the work is deemed to be poor, rightly or wrongly, then it is embarrassing to tell the researcher this, and the most normal reaction is to dodge the responsibility of discussing it and instead not to give that person any more work in the future.

Both these actions are not satisfactory. In the former case it does not recognize that researchers are human too, that they have dedicated a part of themselves to the company for a period of time and therefore have an identification with the work that is more than just a simple financial transaction. In the case when the researcher is deemed to have done poor work, feedback should be carried out so that the researcher can gain some idea why the people in the company came to this view. As was mentioned earlier (this is developed in later chapters), work may be deemed to be poor simply to discredit it as part of the political games that are almost always present in any social organization and may be particularly strong on a particular job. When this is the case, it is especially difficult to go to the researcher and explain the reasons for their work appearing poor. There are cases where the work is poor, and the effect is that money, and worse, time have been wasted. Under these circumstances, it seems fairly obvious that the job failed, and there seems little point on the part of the commissioner of going through it all. This is not to say that the process should still not take place.

The feedback can be as simple as thanking the researcher and complimenting him or her on the work – no more than good manners really. A further way of giving feedback is to tell the researcher of the outcome of the work: the immediate decision that has been taken, or later on, the longer-term consequences. This latter input, although very much welcomed by the researchers, is actually a lot more difficult to manage by the commissioner than might be expected, as often a lot of time has passed, the world has moved on and the researcher and the work are simply out of mind. A simple, but rare, way of doing this is to include regular suppliers on the circulation of any company newspaper or magazine in which new products or changes are reported. This means that not only are they informed about the company, which will help them in subsequent briefings, but they will be able to see what happened as a result of their research.

PARTNERSHIP RELATIONSHIP

There is much talk in the research community about building partnership between suppliers and buyers. This is an interesting phenomenon because what exactly do we mean by the term 'partnership'? Clearly, in the case where an end-user has a close and lasting relationship with a single supplier who becomes as much a confidant and consultant as a researcher, then the relationship is a partnership – and there are many of these. Bur what about the case where a large tracking study has been placed with a supplying company with the expectation that it will be in place for a number of years – is this a partnership, or simply a commercial relationship?

The word 'partnership' suggests an amount of commonality of aim and mutual gain. Essentially it should provide for greater efficiency in handling the interface, which results in lower costs for the supplier and therefore lower costs for the buyer. Greater efficiency can come from a myriad of little things being better: for example, the cost of proposing must be cheaper because it always leads to a job. If money is liberated by the efficiency of the relationship, then some of this money can also be used to make the service better.

However, running such a relationship has to be done with care. It is very easy for one partner to start taking the other for granted, to lose sight of the real reason for the relationship being for *mutual* benefit. This could take the form of the buyer company always calling in people from the agency, whether their presence is necessary or not, or the supplier not passing on cost advantages as lower prices or as better service.

Given that it is possible to run the relationship in a way that means there is money available, this should translate into it actually being nicer to work with one another than with other people. This 'niceness' (which should be seen as a bonus) comes from knowing one another and respecting each other's points of view. But it also carries other responsibilities, like the agency really pulling the stops out on occasions (such as when the client has made a mistake and needs 'rescuing') and the buyer really having a sympathetic understanding of what the backroom people actually have to do to turn round stuff fast.

Ideally, the two organizations should sort of merge, with some interchange of staff taking place, and franker, more open conversation taking place, just as the individuals work with internal colleagues. To achieve all this, and for the relationship to last over a long time, requires a lot of work, commitment and goodwill. There are a number of examples of this happening, and it would be to everyone's advantage if it were to happen more.

CONCLUSION

The relationship between the buyer and the supplier is much more important in the case of qualitative research than it is in quantitative research, and therefore the placing of business is different. This is due to the importance of ensuring a compatibility of personalities, as this is the medium through which the findings of the researcher are transmitted. Therefore the researcher implicitly becomes part of the research design (see Chapter 8) in a way that would be unimaginable in the case of quantitative research. Relationships are necessary two-way, and often the researcher will be relating to a market research department, which may be strong and performing a positive role, or occasionally weak and getting in the way. At their best, market research departments facilitate the growth of information and knowledge within their company, teaching good practices and maintaining a historic view of the market and brands against which the future may be contexted (see Chapter 4), and therefore leverage each piece of research as it is done. Bad research departments make everything more inefficient and get in the way.

6 The nature and scope of quantitative data

The single most important question to ask before going about designing research (and where a great deal of probing is necessary in the briefing session) is whether the research should be built round qualitative or quantitative methods. Given the 'positive' nature of people who commonly populate the business world, the basic underlying thinking is that quantitative data is more sound and objective and therefore more for the 'serious work', while qualitative data is in some way soft and subjective. This strongly held, but often unstated, view is quite wrong, and the purpose of this chapter and Chapter 7 is to explore the nature of these two primary types of data and show that, while in one respect they are very different, when it comes to applying them they have great similarities. This chapter focuses on quantitative data, reviewing the various types that are available and the uses to which they are put. A particular point is made that the so-called 'objective information' that is often associated with the process of market analysis or quantitative research is anything but this, and that the findings are often surrounded by ambiguity.

KEY POINTS

■ Quantitative data comprises internal production and sales data, externally purchased market size and structure data, and a whole variety of tracking and ad hoc quantitative market research studies.

■ Internally generated data is steeply on the increase due to the spread of computerized systems and the growth of online Internet ordering.

■ The internal data and external market size data are typically analysed in different ways for different functions in the business. This means that no coherent view of the way the business is performing is readily available, and this confusion may be compounded by internal politics.

■ Detailed analysis of this data to evaluate performance and identify market movements and their possible causes is very difficult because of the number of factors at play at any one moment.

■ There are, therefore, real ambiguities in the results of this type of analysis (which is not generally accepted) and it is easy for myths to be created which are supposed to be rooted in fact.

■ Apart from the many complexities that lie within the analysis of quantitative data, the situation is worsened by the tendency to analyse quantitative market research data on a question-by-question basis. This means that respondents are not treated as whole objects, and much information is therefore lost. Quantitative market research data generally lacks insight because it is not analysed in a holistic way.

■ However, there is clear evidence that quantitative research is being more 'holistically' analysed and being integrated with other information. This is really a move to applying qualitative methods of analysis to different quantitative data sets.

■ The future could involve moving to a position where companies view the world primarily through their own data, with carefully selected surrogates calibrated by quantitative market research. This could be the *new quantitative*.

■ The changes that are happening to the way that quantitative data is being handled (which seem to be linked to a shift in the values of society) will probably require the MRS Code of Conduct to be revisited to remove potential confusion as to what the industry actually is.

COMPETING PARADIGMS

The dominant analytical philosophy at the moment appears to be the *scientific* one, generally referred to as *modernism*. This has reigned for at least 300 years, and the publication of Newton's *Principia* in 1687 is often taken as a convenient watershed. However, it is impossible to pinpoint with historical accuracy a change of this type, as clearly the scientific method did not suddenly appear with all its trappings, but emerged over a period of time.

Kuhn (1962) writes about the notion of *paradigms*, self-consistent sets of values and ideas that are used to understand the world. He also, importantly, writes about the idea of *competing paradigms* where – to take a biblical analogy – the established paradigm (Goliath) is fought by a newly emerging one (David). The critical point here is that the two paradigms, being self-consistent, can exist happily together if each denies the validity of the other. The fight is actually about getting adherents, and as we know, the *modernist* approach (that is, the scientific approach) successfully replaced its predecessor of the medieval age, which could be termed the *pre-modern era*. At this moment, modernism itself is being generally criticized as being too limiting, and there is a growing body of thought marshalling under the notion of *post-modernism* (Harvey, 1995). This is essentially 'not modernism', a denial of the formal structures of cause and effect that western society has lived with for so long, and as such is not a real paradigm in the terms that Kuhn originally meant. However, it seems obvious that the ground is clear for a new paradigm to emerge.

The market research industry itself can be seen to have a very distinct differentiation between two competing *research* paradigms, those of quantitative and qualitative research (Hussey and Hussey, 1997). In part this can be seen to be a reflection, in microcosm of general social values. Quantitative research is the dominant paradigm – the 'Goliath' – while qualitative research is in the emerging one – the 'David'. Put in this way, qualitative research could be seen to be associated with the movement towards post-modernism, although because this term has now attracted such a lot of negative baggage, many qualitative researchers would not be happy with this association.

However, philosophically it is quite helpful to think of it in this way. As quantitative research is a product of modernism, as is much of western society, it fits well, while qualitative research fits uncomfortably.

This is why people feel very unhappy about taking big business decisions based only on qualitative research.

Another negative consequence of qualitative research being aligned to post-modernism is that judgements about qualitative research are made on the basis of the dominant paradigm; qualitative research tends to be viewed through the spectacles of quantitative research. This is not very helpful or informative because the very basis of the paradigm idea is that the sets of values of one are mutually exclusive of the other. It also perpetuates the notion that there is something not quite right about qualitative research.

FORMATION OF THE MARKET RESEARCH INDUSTRY

Market research started in the United States at about the turn of the 20th century and possibly even earlier. It had a close relationship with the advertising industry, and involved itself with sales and market size, and also, of course, opinion polling. In the United Kingdom, market research was being conducted at least as early as 1923 (Downham, 1993), and appears to have arrived from America. However, there was already a growing tradition for conducting social surveys in the United Kingdom, which started in the late 1800s (Morris, 1996).

Although the majority of market research conducted in the early days was quantitative, ethnographic studies were being conducted in the 1930s by 'Mass Observation', and there was some evidence that Lazarsfeld (Catterall, 2001) was conducting qualitative research in the United States at this time in the form of 'one-to-one' interviews – as he had previously done in Vienna.

The Market Research Society was founded in the United Kingdom in the mid-1940s based on a wish to ensure that proper standards were used. There is some evidence that one of the driving forces for this was the growth in quantitative studies by advertising agencies that were using leading questions to establish 'truths' (Morris, 2001). This emphasis on high quality standards was strongly influenced by the quantitative social research tradition (particularly from the London School of Economics) in the United Kingdom, and the very low level of qualitative research done (if any), meant that it was not taken into consideration during this time of laying down the principles of the profession of market research.

Therefore, market research became defined as 'objective science' in the eyes of its practitioners, and as such, fell into the mainstream era paradigm. It was built around large surveys, with a lot of attention to the statistics of the sample, the 'objectivity' of the questions, and the rigorous application of statistical methods in establishing the 'validity' or otherwise of a difference.

What this inevitably meant was that objectivity, transparency and scientific rigour became particularly elevated characteristics. Market research, therefore, adopted all the trapping of a fully-fledged science (or at least tried to), and protected this idea through the medium of the Code of Conduct of the MRS. These early ideas are still strongly present in the Code and its thinking today.

Furthermore, these early concerns of the founders of the Market Research Society have influenced thinking across Europe (through ESO-MAR) and most of the rest of the English-speaking world (through the former British colonies).

QUANTITATIVE DATA

It follows that quantitative data is held in high regard by society in general and business in particular and is central to the concept of what market research actually is. The following sections examine the different types of quantitative data available to businesses, and challenge the belief about its objectivity, the primary reason for its elevated position.

The classic position is that data analysis is spread across three separate functions. These are the finance function (which deals, not surprisingly, with financial data), the market analysis function (which deals primarily with internal sales and production data, and probably externally purchased market data) and the market research function (which deals with the commissioning and management of externally produced market research data).

Although this chapter has been written in the context of a commercial company, the situation has very strong parallels in the not-for-profit sectors, where very similar factors and ambiguity exist. The 'market' data then features such things as crime rate, benefit uptake, hospital waiting lists and so on. External market figures can come from surveys or panels, such as the British Crime Survey, the Family Expenditure Survey or even the Census, and large-scale one-off ad hoc studies can be done to get a 'market' measure, for example the 'market' for child abuse (Brooker and Cawson, 2001).

We will look at the role of market analysis first, then examine the significance of the emerging 'new data', and finally examine how external quantitative market research fits into the picture.

MARKET ANALYSIS

Market analysis is primarily about the analysis of internally generated data such as production and sales information. This is generally put into the context of information about the market as a whole, which is normally bought in. These total market figures can be obtained from audit figures, industry data pooled with a third party, and sometimes from consumers via panels or straight surveying. A characteristic of these complementary sources of information is that they tend to exist as 'time series', and this gives them particular meaning and utility. As will be shown, market analysis is difficult and, perhaps more to the point, ambiguous in its findings. This is not to say that it is not a valuable activity for a company to engage in, but that it is not as objective as it may seem.

Market analysis is difficult and ambiguous

Market analysis is very difficult and the findings, although based on real 'objective' data, contain ambiguity. Furthermore, the very comprehensive nature of market analysis raises a real problem of 'seeing the wood for the trees'. The difficulty of market analysis is not because of the many technical issues, such as data integrity and the problems that go with the profession of being an analyst, but due to features that are an intrinsic part of doing it. These are:

- The market structure is generally complex, and more so in mature markets.
- The derived measures are many, and different business stakeholders focus on different measures and so derive a different view of the market and its changes.

■ The ability to intellectually or mathematically model the market to understand the impact of events on it is extremely difficult and verges on the impossible.

These three aspects of markets and how they are approached will be expanded in the next three sections.

The complexity of a market

Companies sell their products through a series of channels of trade, such as multiple grocers, through independents, directly and so on, and each of these channels has its own characteristics, and in fact may have its own product range. A given product can be sold in a variety of formats, such as pack types or sizes and whether it carries a promotion or not, and this can fundamentally alter what the product actually is – people can use products in small packs in very different ways from the way they use large packs. Products are sold in different regions that could be as small as a few square miles (a salesperson's territory), marketing regions (often television company areas), countries and even continents or global regions.

The measures of the market are many

The measure of sales is diverse: it can be by numbers of packs, weight or volume, sales value (which may be discounted or not) and even gross profit. These figures can be presented in absolute terms, as a percentage change over a previous period, as a moving total of some description or as a percentage share of a market.

Companies have historic strengths and weaknesses by geography, channel, product category or format. This means that the comparison of one company to another is not strictly comparing like to like. Hence it can be very difficult to compare one company with its competitors or to make real judgements whether it is getting relatively better or not. Although the data is very factual indeed, the messages that come out of it can be confusing.

Impact analysis

All the market and sales data is ultimately historic evaluative data – measures of what has happened. Sometimes what has happened is due to some activity on the part of the company or its competitors; sometimes it is due to external factors, which may be planned – for example, the World Cup – or unexpected – for example, BSE – and sometimes the market is in a general state of growth or decline for unspecified reasons, perhaps economic or social.

Much market analysis is about assessing the size of what has happened in order to evaluate the significance of it. Has a government communication programme impacted on the uptake of a benefit? Has there been any increase in sales due to a particular advertising campaign, direct marketing or promotional activity? What benefit or otherwise has come from one-off events such as the Olympics, or a spell of bad weather? The reasons for conducting such analysis are many. Has the campaign paid for itself? Has this promotion actually shifted more volume? What damage has resulted from something a competitor has done? Is the impact of a one-off event concealing some other trend in the data?

Market analysis is intrinsically ambiguous

Not only is market analysis difficult because of the way that markets work (as explained above), it is also intrinsically ambiguous. This is a very difficult idea to grasp because market analysis is generally based on absolute fact, and by implication it should be possible to arrive at conclusions that are clear and 'factual'. Unfortunately, this is not the outcome in many cases, no matter what the skill of the analysts is. This is because the whole situation in the market is dynamic, and there are generally a multiple of potential effects operating at any one time. Some are favourable to the brands' sales, others are unfavourable and yet others could have an effect either way. For example, is the increase in graffiti simply a demographic effect as a result of there being more children in the age range that does it, or is there something more interesting happening?

The following sections will attempt to show the nature of the ambiguity of market analysis by building on some of the points that have been made earlier.

Econometric modelling only works sometimes

The conventional way of addressing these issues of impact is through *econometric modelling*. This seeks to estimate the magnitude of any effect and to formulate this into an equation. In practice this needs a great deal of information about the performance of the market under different conditions, and there is rarely enough data available to do the job as well as it could be done. This is not the fault of the method but of the complexity of a marketplace, which many are also trying to manipulate.

For example, perhaps the World Cup is being played at the same time as a new ad campaign for a brand breaks. Both events last for a similar time and the brand's home country is knocked out in the third week. Let us suppose that the World Cup is expected to suppress the sales of the brand, and what is seen across this period is no initial change in sales, then a slight increase after three weeks. Does this mean that the ad campaign has had a positive effect? And if so, by how much? Obviously, it can be argued that without the advertising, sales would have fallen, but can anyone really be sure that the World Cup worked against sales as it had been expected to? Perhaps a judgement can be made on this by looking at what happened last time the World Cup happened. Last time the brand's sales did indeed go down, but it is noticed now that this period coincided with a competitor engaging in a heavy price-deal promotion. Perhaps the idea that the World Cup does have an influence is a cultural myth. So the uncertainty continues, analysis leads to analysis, and eventually data or time or patience run out. Other problems also serve to confuse the issue. For example, the supplier for the market data might have changed, and comparability over time becomes compromised. Furthermore, it is actually quite difficult to collect all the information about what is happening in the market, and to do this retrospectively becomes many times more difficult. It cannot even be taken for granted that a company is sure of the price of its own products at any particular time.

So it can be seen that a very simple evaluation of the market in terms of what has influenced it is a lot more difficult than might at first be supposed.

Market structure and dynamics analysis

It was mentioned earlier in this chapter that there are many impacts on the market, and this means that getting a coherent view on what is happening (and therefore a strategy for the future) could be difficult. For example, within a static market one small part could be growing fast, a fact that is concealed because another larger part is declining. What is the implication of this? Is the company's brand in that part that is growing or that which is declining slowly? Are these changes actually due to that particular brand? Is there a threat or is there an opportunity? What could it be? Such analysis could easily lead to further research being commissioned which could be entirely misplaced if the analysis has a flaw.

The beauty of market analysis is in the eye of the beholder

As was referred to earlier in this chapter, there are many measures of a market. This is because different business functions look at the market in different ways. Consequently, market analysis is used differently by the different functions in the company. The finance function will compare the actual sales turnover with a budgeted figure, because the expenditure of the company has been planned against those budgeted sales. Production will think in terms of volume and whether it has the capacity to meet it, and retail buyer will be looking (in market terms) at the popularity of the items or brands that are being proposed to them, in order to ensure that their shops have a proper range of 'quality' products for sale to customers. The operations management may be looking at sales per store and whether they are up over last year, and marketing will be looking at market share and its change over time.

Depending on the way the data is used, people in the company will react differently. For example, the sales are up over last year but not so much that the sales forecast will be reached. What implications does this have on the projected profitability of the company? Should some proposed plant investment be postponed, should the marketing be increased or cut entirely, can the deals that have been struck with suppliers be honoured, and what does it mean if they are not? Is the failure to achieve budget 'our fault' or that of the market? If so, what are the implications for the future? And so on.

THE EMERGING 'NEW DATA'

As has been said earlier, companies have a lot of information, and so far attention has been focused on the problems of handling the classic market analysis data.

Since the introduction of the PC on a wide scale, individual departments have been compiling information relevant to their needs, and often this takes the form of a spreadsheet. Organizations have increasingly demanded that their recruits to management should be numerate, and this combined with the fact that much information now resides on computer has led to a growth of departmental analysis – no longer is analysis the province of the specialist. This development has also to be put in the context of the general business culture, which applauds the use of numbers to justify actions.

The sort of extra analysis that is taking place is very diverse: for example, on financial data, customer-originated data such as 'returns', complaints or information from customer helplines, staff data such as staff turnover rates, sickness and so on, delivery and ordering data such as 'out of stocks' and, increasingly, information from company Web site usage or its particular use in placing an order and tracking it. In addition there could be mystery visitor data, routine operational reports and so on – the list is endless.

Actually, the availability of internally generated information is also on the increase from company-wide systems, rather than just departmental ones. Although computer systems have been employed increasingly to run different aspects of organizations for some years, the data that they could implicitly capture has often not been available for analysis. This is because the people responsible for designing the IT systems used for running the company have historically not been sympathetic to designing the systems to be useful for data analysis – they have had more taxing matters on their minds. However, there are signs that this is changing, and that a more modern and enlightened view is increasingly being taken. The net effect of all this is that more and more information will be becoming available. Obviously, this opens up real opportunities, where companies are prepared to put in the investment necessary, but also further opens up the possibility of data indigestion.

Responsibility for analysis of the new data: the new quantitative

As can be seen, having the ability to conduct comprehensive market analysis is of great value to a company, but it is neither easy to do nor ultimately necessarily unambiguous. The issue that is emerging with the new data is that the analysis of it, such as is taking place, is mostly not in the hands of professional analysts. Furthermore, departments can be quite jealous about giving access to their information to others in the organization, and system-wide data is generally not available at the moment. Consequently, there is a real problem that the increasingly available new information will not be used to the advantage of an organization, simply because of politics and lack of recognition as to the complexities of undertaking such a task. Furthermore, due to the competing perspectives that the different analyses give on the organization, the problem is likely to be a breaking up of the information climate, which is really bad when the company wishes to take strategic decisions. Broadly speaking, an entity in the organization needs to take control of all this, and in part this is what the new 'customer insight departments' could be all about.

Because internal information is abundant and cheap and external information is limited and expensive, it would seem sensible to examine how internal measures can be used as *surrogates* for real customer information, and external market research used to calibrate these surrogates.

Ultimately, this will occur by the application of mathematical methods, many of which are really quite simple. The need will be to use the internal measures as surrogates for consumer behaviour or thinking. For example, the levels of product returns are a direct indicator of unhappiness with the product, but what do different levels of return actually mean in terms of the users' relationship to the brand, and are these returns coming from different people or from the same people? Obviously, consumer research can be used to calibrate this. Furthermore, the rate of change of the level of returns could be used as an indicator of a sudden effect. This could be as simple as the product having a defect that had not been picked up in production, or more interestingly, that the market expectations had suddenly changed, perhaps by the launch of a product by a competitor that has changed the perception in the market.

A very simple way of dramatically levering a simple internally generated figure is to link consumer behavioural data to sales data. A powerful example of this can be illustrated by a retailing case. When a retailer counts the number of sales that it has made, this is not the same as the number of customers it has, as some may have purchased on a number of different occasions. The way to calculate the number of customers is to divide the sales transaction data by the mean frequency of customers, a figure that can easily be obtained from simple research. By linking a survey to the actual transactions it is possible to divide the sales across customers of varying frequency, and those who have shopped for the first time. Doing this on a regular basis means that the numbers and values of customers can be tracked over time. So, for example, the effect of advertising can readily be monitored – after a campaign, the number of new customers would be expected to rise, the frequency of well-known customers might increase, the mean spend of certain frequency groups might change and so forth. Simply asking every 'nth' customer at the till about his or her frequency of visit and entering this data into the till could transform the understanding of the sales performance of a retail chain. Opportunities of this type are many, and is one of the reasons that quantitative research is going into a new period of importance.

It is probably true to say that those companies that embrace these ideas both fully and formally and who focus their attention on building up good pictures from internal data and augmenting it with market research are likely to be the winners in the future. One might even give it a name: 'the new quantitative research'.

So we can expect to see increasing attention being paid to the growing amount of non-classical internal data, and the analysis of it being subsumed into the insight departments where it can be put alongside classical market research and market analysis and its value augmented by consumer calibration. Achieving this will be a real battle for the future – and a bloody and political one it will be too.

CHARACTERISTICS OF QUANTITATIVE MARKET RESEARCH DATA

Typically, the market research department has the role of commissioning and managing external quantitative data, although the exception, as has been mentioned earlier, tends to be market data that is also often managed through a market analysis function.

Quantitative market research has certain positive and negative characteristics which affect how it is analysed. On the positive side it produces a 'big picture', which is easy to communicate and which generates confidence. The problems appear at a more detailed level. These are that quantitative research collects information about individuals but in general fails to analyse it in this way; that the data is produced by humans and is perception data; and finally that much of the data inter-correlates, meaning that much of it is redundant. These are examined in detail next.

Strengths of quantitative market research data

Quantitative research is very helpful in many ways: it is good at showing market sizes, structure and dynamics in terms of both the products that are sold and the segmentation in consumer terms. This information is clearly important for the company to be able to put its overall strategy in context. Quantitative data is also good in terms of the evaluation of products, especially in their overall attractiveness, and to a certain extent data can help with pack evaluation, for example, in speed of brand recognition. In terms of brands, they are useful for measuring the extent of usage, who uses them, how well they are rated and what people think about them in terms of image statements. The output of a quantitative survey can also be expressed in bite-sized statements, such as 'the market grew by 15 per cent last year', and such information is easily retained and used to put decisions in context. Quantitative research is therefore helpful in nailing down certain 'facts' in a way that is generally accepted as true. This reduces the range of debate that takes place in a company, and this is a positive thing as it helps the company to focus better and not to become cluttered up with 'red herrings'.

Potential weaknesses in quantitative data

Analysis tends to be non-holistic

A feature of ad hoc quantitative studies are that they tend to be analysed question-by-question – such and such a proportion of people said 'yes' to this question and so forth. Analysis takes the form of seeing significance in these straight counts. The disadvantage of this is that the holistic nature of an individual is essentially being denied. Analysis is also carried out by comparing the counts of one group of respondents with another, and this can begin to flesh out the meaning, and help to give it a human face, though only in a crude stereotypical way. The sorts of comparisons that are made include 'usage' (compare frequent to infrequent users or to non-users), demographic (compare ABs to DEs) and, less commonly, attitude.

There are techniques that help in looking at an individual in terms of his or her answers to a set of questions. Typically this is called a 'segmentation' exercise, in which respondents are allocated to some type of group. These classification methods generally are based on taking a set of attitudinal and behavioural data scales, transforming them onto a common scale by, for example, standardizing them, pruning the redundant scales (that is highly inter-correlated scales) by examination of the inter-correlation matrix or by factor analysis, and then submitting the whole to cluster analysis and deciding (by inspection) how many clusters are present. The process is very subjective and is hugely dependent on the scales used. However, this can be helpful in getting into segmentations of the market (assuming that there really are such groups), but can fall down when a company seeks to identify the groups in order to market to them.

An alternative method is to apply similar methods to census and related data to identify and apply common social structures in small areas, and attribute some form of consequential market behaviour to them. This method, called geodemographics, has the advantage of not only characterizing and classifying the market segments, but telling a marketer *where* potential customers actually live. This can be of great value for direct marketing activity (direct mail, leaflet drops, poster sites and so on) and for deciding on store locations for retailers.

A more direct method (Callingham and Baker, 2002) is to use the idea of *demographic clusters*. This is simply a three-way table of age, sex and social class with the cells populated with whatever information is relevant. This takes into account that the standard methods of analysis, which analyse by sex, age and wealth (social class) separately, fail to recognize that a young man is different from a young woman. The problem of using demographic clusters is one of economy: that is, depending upon how the tables are constructed, there could be over a hundred cells. This would need a survey of over 10,000 to populate the cells, and this would normally be too expensive. However, with the recent advent of Internet survey methods, large sample sizes are becoming more of a possibility.

The use of such a system has many advantages. First, the groups are understandable as they are the groups that we normally use in everyday life to interpret people. Second, the major media surveys are of a size that mean that they can be analysed by these groups, and third, in principle it would be possible to obtain counts of these groups in small geographical areas from the census for direct marketing and retail purposes.

Another way in which combinations of questions are used together is to form a mathematical relationship between the questions at the individual level, for example the response to price. This can enable an expected response to a variety of situations that were not formally asked about in the questionnaire to be calculated for each individual, and then summed across them all to get at an overall population response. This type of approach accepts the individual nature of a respondent, but of course assumes that the basic mathematical model is sound.

Quantitative research is not really objective

One of the implicit claims of quantitative research is that it has some form of objectivity about it, which gives it an aura of greater truth than qualitative research. However, it is well known that the way that a respondent will answer a question will vary depending upon how it is asked and the context in which it is embedded. In addition, respondents, who are not objects but thinking beings, will try to work out the purpose of the survey, and this can influence how they answer: for example, with questions on pay in an employee survey. Furthermore, respondents, being polite social entities, will try their best to answer the questions asked, no matter how silly they are, and of course cannot answer questions that are not asked, even if they would have been of great importance.

Halo effects can be rife

Much of the investigations conducted in market research are actually on topics that are not of great importance to the respondent, and which they have not thought about much. Respondents can therefore hear many of the questions simply in terms of 'is it good or is it bad?' and answer accordingly. This results in there being considerable correlation between the question answers, which produces a 'halo effect', and can make interpretation more difficult and uncertain.

This can be particularly evident in questions about how 'important' a series of aspects of a product or concept are – a respondent may say that they are all important! Attempts can be made to counter this by asking questions in a series of ways so that the importance of each part of the concept or brand can be estimated for each respondent. Such questions may seek to force the respondent to 'trade off' one thing against another, and results in a series of derived variables that characterize a person, and that can then be subject to further analysis (Baker and McDonald, 1999). There is an implicit assumption here that the differences in the importance of the various aspects of the product are of sufficient meaningfulness to be worth measuring, and also that the choices are made in a linear way.

Other ways of judging importance include the emerging 'latent' methods. In these, regression-type equations are derived and the coefficients of the independent variables used as the basis of measures of their importance. Increasingly, analysis of this type is moving from a 'global' one (where one equation is obtained from the whole data set) to 'local', where a number of equations are derived from subsets of the data.

THE TYPES OF QUANTITATIVE MARKET RESEARCH DATA

This type of quantitative data can be thought of as dividing into 'tracking studies' and 'bespoke studies'.

Quantitative market research tracking studies

Advertising tracking

Much of the external data a company buys is quantitative data that represents the market through the eyes of the consumer, and increasingly this is being monitored continuously. The tracking of the effect of advertising, for example, is quite common ('Our brands are our most important asset' – see Chapter 2) and the purpose is to get some justification for very large marketing spends. Marketing is one of the largest 'discretionary' lines on the budget, and is very easy to cut when times get hard without there being much immediate obvious impact. The tracking of its effect at least allows a debate to be conducted as to the effectiveness of a particular campaign, and the theoretical opportunity to learn from mistakes.

Customer and staff satisfaction tracking studies

Other important tracking studies, which may or may not be continuous, are the tracking of customer satisfaction (for those businesses that have customers – 'Our customers are our most important asset' see Chapter 2), and measures of the staff satisfaction ('Our staff are our most important asset'). The custodians of these different studies tend to be different functions (marketing, operations and human resources respectively), and it is not often that analysis of either of them takes place with the other in mind.

Tracking studies are not all they claim to be

Tracking studies have been very much in vogue over the last 15 years. Their advantages are that they give a *continuous* feedback about whatever is being measured, that they do not suffer from the many things that can have impact on research that is based on only a short period of field work (such as very bad weather or a strike of some sort), and that they can also display seasonal effects if they are present in the market.

Unfortunately, they are complex to report and analyse (in the same way that market measures are) and they can also be very boring. Customer satisfaction surveys, for example, show little movement wave by wave, and the only thing more boring than one straight line is a lot of them (Hannah and Brand, 1999)! Advertising tracking is more exciting.

As a general rule, too much is expected from most tracking studies, and insufficient further analysis of them within market segments is conducted to give further insight. They tend not to give the 'early warning' that they are often sold on, and such signs as they do give tend to be ignored or 'explained away' for company and socio-political reasons.

Bespoke quantitative market research studies

Other major external quantitative data collection can take place with the testing of products (though less of this takes place now than formerly), testing of packs (particularly for global brands) and usage and attitude studies (U&As). The latter attempts to quantify who is using which brands and how they perceive them (their image).

Experience shows that the image of brands seems to be remarkably stable over time (and indeed country – see Chapter 3) when measured in this way. U&As are an area where there has been growing dissatisfaction, due mainly to the very small movements they show over time, and the difficulty of interpreting the figures in an unambiguous way. Naturally, the purpose of marketing is, in many cases, to achieve exactly this, a static position for the brand (that is, not a declining one), but few marketing people would emotionally accept this – they want it to get better.

A number of innovative quantitative products have appeared

recently on the market, which attempt to enliven these types of studies. These may use new methods of constructing the image battery to be more relevant to an underlying theory, cleverer ways of categorizing the level of loyalty that the consumers have to a brand, or the classification of consumers into intuitively recognizable 'social value' groups. Subsequent analysis of the data is then done on the relevant terms.

U&As are often initially conceived as a one-off study, but there is a tendency to repeat them every one or two years, and in international companies to spread the form of the initial U&A to new countries and regions. The reason for this is to have comparability across time and place, and this is clearly a sensible thing to do. It is also good news for the initial research supplier who naturally is the first port of call for the 'repeats' and the 'extensions'.

Unfortunately, there is a downside to this – the study can get into a historical straitjacket. Furthermore, the original design of the study might have been different had this further use of it been envisaged. Things that change over time include the brand list and required sample, both of which are pretty fundamental. However, there can also be more insidious and potentially important changes occurring. These involve the nature and the structure of the market, which if not incorporated can cause the view given by the study to be distorted. Such changes may include the growth of an alternative market that is addressing the same basic needs, but whose competitive power is not being monitored. This can be particularly damaging as such a market may grow up quietly to become, after a few years, a major threat that has largely passed unnoticed or at least has been ignored.

SUMMARY OF QUANTITATIVE RESEARCH

Quantitative research is therefore commissioned within the dominant 'modernism' paradigm in the belief that it will produce objective data and analysis of it will produce an objective finding – the 'truth'. This outcome is clearly not forthcoming in those cases where there is any complexity in the market, and to that extent there is almost a conspiracy of silence.

There is a growing awareness of all this which is sometimes shown up in the sense of disillusionment that can surround market research, and some people are moving fairly quickly away from the straitjacket of the scientific paradigm. These people are bringing a more holistic approach to the business of analysis which is more in keeping with the qualitative approach (this will be expanded in the next chapter). At its best this approach works extremely well, but at its worst it mixes the paradigms and can confuse the recipient, leading to debates about validity and reliability, which are mostly unhelpful at the time that one is looking at some results.

This is therefore a difficult time for quantitative researchers as the rules for analysis are changing and this brings with it a sense of uncertainty. Early on in this chapter, the role of the Code of Conduct of the Market Research Society was mentioned, and it seems likely that this Code now needs to be re-examined at a deeper philosophical level in order to bring certainty back.

CONCLUSION

Companies are awash with quantitative information (both internal and external), and this situation is likely to increase in the future as electronic ordering systems come into play and IT management recognize the importance of including data analysis within IT business process project specifications. The analysis of this information is full of difficulty, and the result, unsurprisingly, is ambiguous. The reasons for this are that the variables impacting on the data are complex and often coincident, and also that the different functions in the company look at the data in very different ways, which makes it impossible to create a coherent company-wide view of what is going on.

Quantitative research, though excellent at identifying macro aspects of the market or brand, is ill equipped to address the subtleties of contemporary marketing in which brands are often personified. Recent moves to analyse quantitative data in a more holistic and integrated way will address this problem in part, but will also raise the question as to whether what is being done is scientific. In this context, the real issue is whether anyone still cares whether it is or not. The appearance of consumer insight departments within companies in principle produces the infrastructure for the introduction of a more imaginative use and analysis of quantitative data.

7 Qualitative information and its relationship to quantitative information

Classically, as we all know, the data collection phase of market research is divided into two distinct types, qualitative and quantitative. However, this divide is much more than the technical divide it appears to be, and runs to the heart of market research itself as it is conceptualized by the practitioners in the industry. This chapter develops the ideas referred to in the earlier chapters (especially in Chapter 6), and describes the philosophical differences between the two methodologies and the historical and social reasons that they have the significance they do. It is very clear that the two methods are complementary processes that have quite distinct characteristics, which should logically lead to decisions about their use in any particular case. However, this even-handed view is still not accepted at an emotional level in organizations, and the reasons for this are explored.

KEY POINTS

- The dominant paradigm of this era was the positive scientific one, and quantitative research is its manifestation in the market research world.
- Quantitative research became the main paradigm of the fledging research industry as the result of a variety of historical accidents, and by good chance, was fit for the purpose then required of it.
- Quantitative research is good for counting how many do this or that, and it can do so in a valid and reliable way. However, quantitative research is really a descriptive methodology rather than a scientific one, even though it has sought to use scientific principles.
- Clients work in businesses that presume that the world can be represented numerically; business cases are made and supported with numbers – the more explicit the information is, the better. Hence, there is a natural affinity between the client world and quantitative research.
- The growing sophistication of marketing in the 1960s, in particular the move away from promoting the literal and tangible aspect of the brand as its proposition, meant that the quantitative paradigm increasingly became less able completely to satisfy the needs of marketing. People no longer wanted to know only what the differences were, but also why there were differences.
- Qualitative research is good for producing a logical narrative grounded in the fieldwork that is easy to understand and remember; and one that explains and stimulates too. This made qualitative research more suitable for aspects of brand work than was quantitative research.
- Qualitative research has been growing in importance ever since the 1960s and is now a genuine alternative paradigm, but one that is still fighting to be seen as different from the mainstream era paradigm (modernism). This is why major business decisions are not taken solely on the basis of qualitative research.

THE ESSENTIAL CONFLICT BETWEEN QUALITATIVE AND QUANTITATIVE RESEARCH

The previous chapter showed how the quantitative paradigm came to be the defining one for market research – in that it fitted with the business psychology of justifying everything with numbers – but suggested that its supposed objectivity is little more than an illusion. However, there is no doubt that the thriving qualitative industry is also well accepted. If the two methods are equally evident, surely this means that their status must be similar, and that business is not just working under principles of modernism. To an extent this is true, and certainly there have been shifts over time, but the fact remains, and needs to be explained, that no major business decisions are made on qualitative research alone.

The next sections examine the rise of qualitative research and explain the conflicts that lie at the heart of using it – basically that it delivers the 'goods' where quantitative research cannot, but that unfortunately it is not numbers based and is still viewed with caution.

Quantitative research was perfect for the job – in the 1950s

In Chapter 2, the point was made about how people tended to gravitate into functions that worked with the type of knowledge (explicit or tacit) they felt most comfortable with. On the whole, people who relate best to explicit knowledge tend to be the people who run business communities. Such people include accountants, buyers, engineers, operational management (including managing directors) and so on. Of course, explicit knowledge is by definition historic knowledge, as otherwise how could it be written down? Quantitative surveys produce hard factual (and historic) information, which appeals to these types of people, and with which they also feel comfortable.

In the early days of market research, the sorts of problems that needed to be addressed tended to be quite literal in nature. They took the form of behavioural studies, opinion polling and large amounts of product testing. Actually, the importance attributed to product testing at that time is difficult to conceive today, but this was driven by the need of the advertising industry to be able to make strong product claims.

Television advertising started in the United Kingdom in the early 1950s, and was the first of its kind in Europe. This gave an impetus to the research industry in the United Kingdom, particularly with respect to product testing. In fact, many of the early research companies were to have their origins in the environment of an advertising agency. The reason for this was that the product propositions that were then advertised tended to be very literal ('Raelbrook Poplin, the shirt you don't iron', 'You'll wonder where the yellow went, when you brush your teeth with Pepsodent', 'It looks good, it tastes good and by golly it does you good' – Mackeson).

The net effect of all this was that the data that was required was very much in the form of straightforward literal facts, and was therefore ideally matched to what the market research industry had to offer at that time.

Quantitative research was not good for the job in the 1960s

In the 1960s, the nature of advertising began to move away from making literal claims to creating images and offering lifestyles. This was probably to do with the growth in the economy in the 1960s, and the increasing difficulty of differentiating products on performance in well established categories. As this happened, the market research industry began to have difficulties with meeting the needs of its customers.

The sorts of business discussions that needed to be informed were infinitely subtler than had formerly been the case. Quantitative research and the people who populated it began to look distinctly rigid and unhelpful. Of course, this was not actually articulated at the time, because it was not understood, but it is from this point that there has been a growing unease with the output of the industry. In effect the current social (quantitative) paradigm was showing signs, for the first time, of not being fit for the job.

This period (the 1960s), as is well known, coincided with big social changes, and in particular was a period associated with the development of new ideas and approaches. The UK's growth had been held back for almost 30 years with the recession of the 1930s, the war of the 1940s and the post-war development period of the 1950s and was, by the 1960s, bursting for change. The 1960s was a time when established values were questioned, and in this environment the possibility of a completely new approach to market research (and to anything else for that matter) was possible. This was fortunate because it was necessary!

Qualitative research comes to the rescue

Commercial qualitative research seems to have been around in the United States before the Second World War with Lazarfeld's and Dichter's names strongly associated with it, and was mainly one-to-one interviewing based on a psychoanalytic tradition. It is believed that is was brought to the United Kingdom in 1958 by Bill Schlackman who was Vice-President of Dichter's Institute of Motivational Research (Imms, 1999). However, there is a reference to the use of a 'psychologist' to help in the development of a questionnaire in a book by Dugdale (1969) about her life in the research industry, which started in 1936.

In hindsight, it can be seen that qualitative market research arrived in the United Kingdom just as the need for it was becoming apparent, and just as the established quantitative paradigm was beginning to be seen to be failing. It also had a very strong evangelist in the form of Bill Schlackman, who was able to sell the merits of this new method of doing market research and build a following. However, this method of research flew in the face of the established paradigm and many people simply could not accept it as being a valid methodology. 'David' had arrived and no one understood him, and the Kuhnian competition of paradigms had started.

Meanwhile, in the United States, the work of Dichter and his Institute of Motivational Research fell into disrepute, probably as a result of his personality. In fact, there seems to have been a backlash to what he was doing, which (from a United Kingdom perspective) held up the development of qualitative research in the United States. For years now, qualitative work in the United States has been very literal and hardly more than semi-structured interviews – or 'focus groups' as they became known.

In the United Kingdom, however, qualitative research grew from strength to strength, having a fertile social environment in which to grow, and a market that increasingly recognized that there was a need for it. In addition, a new breed of qualitative researchers (Goodyear, Cooper, Gordon and so on) who had been trained in psychology rather than psychoanalysis entered and influenced the industry (Imms, 1999).

However, the journey was not achieved easily, and it was with reluctance that quantitative researchers, many of whom were running the large and successful research businesses, bowed to the inevitable and accepted qualitative research as a legitimate form of market research.

An indication of this difficulty is given by the fact that qualitative researchers felt they were not being represented properly by the main professional organization, the MRS, and felt the absence of representation so strongly that they set up a separate organization, the Association of Qualitative Research Practitioners, now the AQR. So, even when qualitative research was at a peak of success it was not fully accepted by the main body of the industry.

QUANTITATIVE RESEARCH AND QUALITATIVE RESEARCH ARE FUNDAMENTALLY DIFFERENT

It is hardly necessary to state that qualitative research differs greatly from quantitative research. The differences at the superficial level are sample size, sample representativeness, and the absence of a structured questionnaire. These differences are often taken as suggesting that qualitative research is less objective (and therefore less true) than quantitative research. Actually, the two methodologies are complementary methods of investigation, and each has strengths where the other is weak and weaknesses where the other is strong.

The fundamental difference is that qualitative research takes the 'whole person' as its starting point, and has as its origins a wish to understand how that person works in terms of his or her relationship with brands and markets. Qualitative research, therefore, involves talking to people in a holistic way whereas quantitative research on the whole does not. This different viewpoint leads to an entirely different way of analysing the results.

In the case of quantitative research the emphasis is on counting the numbers of respondents that do or say this or that. This means that conventional statistical tests can be applied to assess how certain the number arrived at is. Consequently, this methodology puts great emphasis on the sample size and on the representativeness of the sample. All this is fine if the requirement is to know a figure of this type (and this is the strength of quantitative research), but it does not help in understanding anything other than simple relationships (which is its weakness).

Qualitative research does not seek to establish sizes at all, it is much more about the relationship that people have with their surroundings. This means that sample size has no real meaning in the context of qualitative research. What is needed is a representation of the *different views*, not a representative sample of the people. In principle, what is needed is an example of each of the different views and an enquiry approach that elicits these views. This necessarily takes it into detailed and sensitive investigation of individuals, with all the paraphernalia of qualitative methodology. Analysis of the information is nothing to do with statistical reliability, but about the production of a coherent explanation of what has been found. As such, the analytical approach is very much one of induction, which as we will see later in not something that quantitative researchers are good at.

However, as the predominant social and business paradigm is a scientific one, it seems virtually impossible to have a business debate about qualitative findings (when some important crunch point is being reached) without the scientific thinking being raised, with associated implied criticisms. How many people did you interview? Were they representative? And so on.

Barnham (1995), has advocated that it would be more helpful to examine qualitative ideas through the spectacles of the pre-modernism of medieval times, with which he believes it has much in common. Medieval thought took as its primary principle the idea of essences, and that any object was a coincidence of essences that caused it to be instanced. A 'thing', therefore became a consequence of the sum of the essences and importantly of their relationship. To understand the relationships, it was only necessary to examine a sufficient number of instances of the 'thing' to discover what these essences were and what the ranges of these relationships were. From this, the infinite manifestations of it could be divined.

Barnham (1995) argues that this is the process that is, in practice, followed in qualitative brand research – the brand is disassembled and the relationship of the constituent parts worked out. A brand is instanced in people's heads, rather than only being the concrete manifestation that we see on the shelf. Therefore it is only necessary to examine a finite number of these instances, that is, the people in whose heads it exists, in order to work out the range of relationships of the constituent parts. No 'Brownie points' are gained on how many instances are used – they are gained by the profundity of the relationships discovered.

Not everyone will agree with this analysis, although many find it attractive.

Wardle (2001) has made the point that the number of instances required to conduct a qualitative study is not only about achieving the nature of relationships but also about having a sufficiently reasonable chance of coming across an instance (person) that allows all the others to be understood. This is why samples are spread across demographic groups and across the country, not because these layers are expected to be helpful in analysis (as they would be in the case of quantitative research), but that they allow a greater chance of the collective views about the matter in hand being present in the research.

THE CHALLENGES TO QUALITATIVE RESEARCH

As mentioned earlier in this chapter, when crunch time comes and qualitative research is being used to support a particular case, the findings are generally challenged in terms of the scientific paradigm. This section examines those challenges and provides an answer to them.

The debate about the validity and reliability of qualitative research still occasionally crops up. The big questionmarks seem to revolve around sample size and representativeness, researcher interaction with the respondents impacting on the data collected, and the level of 'subjectivity' involved in the subsequent interpretation of the results (Quinn Patton, 1986).

There has been a lot of work looking at the reliability (is the data collected repeatable?) and validity (is the data collected meaningful?) of qualitative research (Robson and Hedges, 1993). Astonishingly, this work was done within the qualitative community, presumably as a counter to the all-pervading quantitative 'Goliath'. The two research methods are in different paradigms (Sykes, 1990), and therefore it is not possible to compare them on a point-for-point basis. For example, questions about representativeness (which is vital for quantitative research and therefore a necessary obsession for quantitative researchers) are meaningless to qualitative researchers, who are more interested in the relationship of the various components, (Barnham,

1995). Furthermore, such questions are unfair to qualitative research and loaded against it. Equivalent 'unfair' questions could be levied against quantitative research, such as 'How do you understand the way in which this question was answered?', which similarly cannot be answered from within the quantitative research paradigm.

As was described earlier, these questions are ultimately meaningless and not therefore actually answerable. A better question to ask is 'Does qualitative research help decision making in a company?', and it seems certain that it does. To this extent it does not matter whether two researchers, given the same brief, come up with identical truths, provided that either version presented has utility. Of course, such a statement is an anathema to those whose thinking is derived from the scientific method, which believes in the god of objective truth.

As we all know, the net effect of this is that qualitative research is more personal and tells a story about people in a way that quantitative research does not. It is easy to assimilate and to comprehend. It gives a simple picture that is rich in detail through which much greater and more profound understanding is achieved. Its very lack of definiteness is full of creative possibilities, and therefore it is an enabler of change.

The complexity of contemporary products, in terms of how they sit in the market, and how they relate to each other and to potential or actual segments in the market, is extremely difficult to capture using quantitative research, simply because quantitative research looks at one bit of it at a time. Qualitative research is the only way of investigating these matters, and finds particular utility in the study of brands and the advertising that supports and makes them. Of course qualitative research is not only used in this way, it is also used in much simpler and pragmatic ways. Typical of this is exploratory work done to help scope the dimensions of a quantitative questionnaire, or work that is done quickly when there is no time to mount a full-scale survey. This fits with the increase in the pace of business.

FAILURES IN QUANTITATIVE RESEARCH

When we look back at the application of the scientific method to market research, as manifest by quantitative research, it can be seen that one critical element of the scientific approach seems to have been missing.

This critical element is actually the only reason for engaging in science, that is, to be able to make predictions about the future.

Practitioners of the scientific approach to market research, as embodied in quantitative market research, have always been extremely reluctant to move away from the factual findings of the survey, yet the scientific approach is fundamentally about building a theoretical framework to explain the world.

Hypotheses, or scientific laws, always have a 'range of convenience', or 'domain', that is the broad area of physical phenomena to which they claim to relate. Very large amounts of academic resource are applied to testing the resilience of a particular theory to predict the future, with the purpose of displaying its weaknesses, and hopefully finding ways of recasting it in a better and more encompassing form. This type of work also attempts to extend the 'range of convenience' of the law.

In the case of the quantitative market research industry, with all its historic concern with rigour, this is not the case, because *no theories have been built*. This is truly astonishing, and may be due to the undue presence of what physical scientists might think of as being pseudo-scientists among the founding fathers of the industry, such as economists and statisticians. Whatever its cause, the tendency to *describe it*, rather than to *explain it* has been a fundamental weakness to the industry as it originally was, and continues to be of quantitative research now.

Many quantitative researchers would claim that the assertion that quantitative researchers do not build theories is not wholly true, especially as there have for many years been attempts to build mathematical models of respondent behaviour, which can be used in a 'what if?' way. Mathematical models are often the best way of capturing the findings of a quantitative study, but they are intrinsically insensitive to the vagaries of the way people think. Just because a person likes a 'this', and separately a 'that', does not mean that when they are provided together he or she likes the combination more. Mathematical models, as created in the research industry, report the actual or claimed behaviours or beliefs of people in a more compact way and thereby make it easier to comprehend a lot of information; but they are essentially descriptive. This is not the same as creating a theoretical framework of understanding, which can only come from induction and then be tested for truth against the facts being collected.

In contrast, qualitative researchers *build theories all the time*. Theory is an important outcome of qualitative research, and is what is liked about it. Theoretical frameworks are also produced when a person is doing a lot of work in one area, either because he or she specializes in that area, or because he or she is in a commissioning environment that necessarily is specialized. In the former case, the individual builds particular expertise. In the latter case, the building of the hypothesis is a fundamental part of creating and orchestrating the information climate of the company – as mentioned in Chapter 2.

Here we have yet another paradox within the industry: those who support and identify with the scientific method appear to be poor at taking it to its ultimate conclusion, while those who have thrown out the scientific tradition seem to be good at it.

Arguably, the creation of a set of consumer theories is the real route to consumer insight.

THE DIFFICULTY OF PRODUCING A THEORY

The creation of a theory is hard *because* it requires induction. Publication of it is also brave, because it is always possible that a piece of information will appear that is in contradiction to the hypothesis. Ironically, this is exactly why true scientists publish. A theory only has a range of convenience, but even when this is very limited, it needs a lot of work to convince oneself and others that it is truly resilient. This takes time and dedication, and is really what the academic world is about.

Induction, being an act of creation is brave, and quantitative researchers tend not to be brave in this respect. They tend to be conservative people who draw comfort from working in a world that is prescribed by facts. They tend to be careful and precise and very disciplined. They have great integrity and stand back from the issues, seeking to be impartial and objective. They are clever, well skilled in the handing of the mechanics of the survey, and enjoy these mechanics. They are also necessarily cautious and in some people's eyes a bit boring. They therefore tend to be *reporters* of other people's news (as comes from a survey) and are reluctant to input their own opinion. After all, they think, they are only *one* person, while the survey summarizes the opinion of *several hundreds* of people. They generally deny that they are in the unique position of having analysed the data, and therefore have a valuable and particular view on that data that no one else will ever get. This is putting aside the fact that they have also analysed large numbers of similar surveys and that their expertise and experience is of value in putting the findings into context.

Qualitative researchers, on the other hand, have an unusual mix within their temperament, many aspects of which could be seen as contradictory. They are intelligent, curious and passionate about the truth, and validate the veracity of the truth through their own conviction of interpretation of evidence that they have personally collected. They are independent minded and able to synthesize original approaches on the basis of their intellect and through actively listening. They are prepared to stand by their findings, which are ultimately grounded in the field-work they have done, and they enjoy 'selling' their findings and changing the way others think about the world, but they are not bombastic or bullying. Indeed they are the reverse, being sensitive to their environment and generally liberal minded, and achieve their end through persuasion. As a group they are very responsive to delivering findings that the client believes and they like to be liked; but the truth still comes first.

With these two stereotypical descriptions, it is obvious that those people who populate the quantitative community are less likely to feel comfortable with the process of induction, and are much happier with deduction. The qualitative researcher, however, will happily construct a theoretical framework to explain his or her findings. The problem is that inventing such things is actually quite easy if the person edits out information that conflicts with it, and this is the underlying fear that people have when listening to qualitative researchers.

Actually, the real difficulty of concluding a qualitative analysis is coming to a point when one feels that a theoretical framework has been arrived at that does encompass all the main information, though necessarily not all of it because some will inevitably be erroneous or wrong. This is the real cross that qualitative researchers have to bear, and it is exactly how they bear their crosses that makes matching personalities between the client and the researcher so much more important in the case of qualitative research than qualitative research. It is also why qualitative researchers need to be left alone while they are doing the analysis (see Chapter 9).

LOOKING FORWARD

There is an amount of disquiet with the market research industry at the moment (Brand and Jarvis, 2000) in that there appears to be increasing concern about what is called 'a lack of *consumer insight'*. As suggested earlier in this chapter, this may be because hypotheses about the market or the consumer are not regularly generated outside of qualitative research. Lack of consumer insight also seems to be related to the number of caveats that a formal market researcher brings to the discussion, which clients tend to think is unhelpful. In part, this comes from adhering too strongly to a particular research paradigm, and there is now more discussion about the notion of *'bricolage'* (combining many unrelated things) and so-called *'informed eclecticism'* (Spackman and Barker, 2000), which is very much about selecting the paradigm that is best for purpose, and then not being limited by it. This is quite a change from the ethos of the early market research industry, and may reflect the fact that the current modernistic paradigm is beginning to lose ground. It also addresses the dilemma of whether to stick with the safe quantitative research and fail to grasp the subtleties of the market, or go to qualitative and risk getting the answer 'wrong'.

Perhaps central to this whole debate is the question that there is somehow an ultimate truth – a question that is regularly visited by philosophers; it is likely that objective truth is an illusion, as will be illustrated next.

The earliest known model to describe the movement of the heavens was the Ptolemaic model, which assumed that the Earth was the centre of the universe. This hopelessly incorrect model served humankind for over a thousand years, giving quite good predictions of planetary movements, though it has been replaced subsequently on a number of occasions. This is not to say that the various theories did not have value in their time, it is certain that they did, but they were not 'true' and it *did not matter* either. Examples of scientific, 'objectively based' models being outmoded are legion. Furthermore, recent developments in chaos theory (Hall, 1993) suggest that the very predictability hoped for from the scientific method is not possible in certain circumstances. This is not because the truth of a relationship is questioned but because the relationship is very sensitive to the initial conditions. In practice, there are occasions when it is not possible to define these starting conditions sufficiently closely for the outcome to lie within an acceptable range of preciseness – change the starting conditions a tiny bit, and the outcome varies greatly. Forecasting of the weather is an example of this. When this is coupled with the Heisenberg uncertainty principle (which crudely means you cannot have your cake and eat it) it means that for many processes that depend on the atomic or microscopic, a common rule can produce dramatically different results. This is why identical twins are never truly identical or why the leaves of a plant are always different, even through an identical biological rule has been applied in their creation. The diversity of nature and evolution depend on objective truths *not* always being true.

In many ways people are increasing thinking about models of the world that are less mechanical and less predictable, and the application of such models to people, although a strongly wished for goal, seems increasingly irrelevant. Within this context, the divide between objective reality (*really* true) and subjectiveness (something *you* think is true – but probably not me) also becomes increasingly irrelevant. But it is this divide that lies at the heart of the divide between quantitative and qualitative research and the associated schism in the industry.

CONCLUSION

Quantitative research has always been a descriptive methodology rather than a scientific one, though it has sought to use scientific principles. It became the main paradigm of the fledging research industry for a variety of historical accidents, and, by good chance, was fit for the purpose required of it. The growing sophistication of marketing, in particular the move away from promoting the literal and tangible aspect of the brand as its proposition, meant that the quantitative paradigm no longer was able to satisfy its needs. People no longer wanted to know only what the differences were, but also why. The social upheaval of the 1960s produced an iconoclastic environment in which the soil was ready for a new methodology to grow. It was the changing needs of the market that provided the nutrients.

The strengths of quantitative research remain clear – it is good for counting how many do this or that, and it can do it in a valid and reliable way. The merits of qualitative research are of producing a logical story grounded in the fieldwork that is easy to understand and remember, and one that explains and stimulates too. Clearly, these two methodologies are complementary.

However, the battle is still not quite resolved. Not only are there still people in the industry who have concerns about the sampling and interpretation methods used for qualitative research, though these are dramatically down in numbers, but also there is still the client to contend with. Clients work in businesses that presume that the world can be represented numerically. This not only applies to the finance function (although this has been an important driving force), but also to almost every other function too. Business cases are made and supported with numbers – the more explicit the information is, the better – and qualitative research has to battles against these very strongly held beliefs.

The great success of qualitative research has been with brands and advertising, where quantitative methods have generally (though not exclusively) proved to be unhelpful. The problem is when there is some contention about the findings and a lot of money is at stake, companies are still very uncomfortable about relying on qualitative research alone and revert to type. This is nothing to do with logic, but with a series of profoundly held beliefs that unfortunately are misplaced and wrong.

8 Designing the research

Market research involves a particular structured way of collecting and interpreting information. The actual 'structure' of data collection is called the ' research design'. The efficacy of the research will ultimately be dependent on the appropriateness of the design, and this means that it is probably the single most important aspect of research (if there is one). No matter how good the elicitation, analysis, interpretation or presentation are, if the basic design is faulty, the real objectives of the research will be unlikely to be met.

The elements of a research design are the objectives, the sample (nature, size and location), methodology used, coverage and stimulus material required, as well as a number of logistical factors such as timing and cost. Of these, the hardest to get right is the definition of the objectives of the research upon which, more than anything, the final output depends. A major problem in getting the objectives properly defined is the lack of quality time that the end-user clients are generally prepared to spend in expressing their problem to the researcher.

KEY POINTS

- The design of the research is a critical stage of the whole process, which if not done well will radically prejudice the outcome of the research.

- The design involves defining the purpose, setting objectives, methodology, sample, investigative area or *coverage*, stimulus material, logistic factors such as timing and cost, and the selection of the agency or researcher to do the work.
- The creation of a good design is hampered by the general poor quality of the research briefing from the end-user client. This includes the difficulty of getting quality time allocated to the briefing, and the difficulty of appreciating the diversity of the different research stakeholders' perspectives, and being able to prioritize them. An additional problem can occur when something critical to the research changes between the design and the debrief, and the researcher is not made aware of it.
- Further problems that impact radically on the design are the assumptions that are brought to it by the client. These are necessary to reduce the scale of the research in order to have realistic costs and timings, but can be very damaging if they are wrong. It is especially damaging when these assumptions or preconceptions lead to fieldwork excluding important categories of respondents or areas of enquiry, as under these circumstances there is no way the relevant information can be obtained.
- In addition to the various client stakeholders, account should also be taken in the design of the different groups involved in actual research. These are: the respondents themselves, the recruiter, the moderator in the case of qualitative research, the person who does the analysis (if different), a whole host of agency support staff, and professional and legal requirements such as the Code of Conduct of the MRS and the data protection legislation.

WHAT A MARKET RESEARCH DESIGN IS

Although it is very difficult to isolate one part of the research process and say that it is the most important part – as the ultimate strength of the research is based on how the whole process is conceived and executed – its design must come near or at the top for importance. The reason for this is that if the design is wrong, then all the other effort is for nought.

What exactly do we mean when we talk about the 'research design' and how does one come into being? Typically, a research design is a description of an approach to creating information that will throw light on a particular problem. The problem itself may be expressed at a number of levels, from the most general to very tightly specified outputs. Typically the design will include what the problem is and what is expected of the research (its purpose and its objectives), and it will select a methodological approach or approaches, and define how they will be used in this case. In particular there will need to be a definition of who is going to be talked to (the respondents), what they are going to be talked to about (essentially the questions), how many respondents will be needed, and whether they need to be stimulated in some way or other (for example, shown a pack, given a product, asked to go and have an experience and so on).

However, there is the matter as to *who* actually does the design, and the answer to this is not as simple as might be thought.

WHO DOES THE DESIGN

In principle, anybody who has both the technical knowledge of market research and the information to understand the problem in hand can produce a research design. In practice, it tends to be a result of a partnership between the client and the researcher, with one side taking the dominant role. Actually, it is almost always foolish for a client, no matter how expert, to foist a design onto a researcher or a research agency, if the best is to be achieved from them. This is because there are many ways of skinning a cat, and the actual agency or researcher that one is talking to will have its own unique body of experience. In the case of individual qualitative researchers, the way that they feel most happy approaching a problem will be different and depend upon themselves as individuals. This means that in the case of qualitative research, part of the design is truly who has been chosen to do the research.

The term 'client' is used a lot in the research industry, but as has already been described, this term covers many different things. The 'client' could be an in-house researcher who is familiar with the actual and political issues at stake in the company and can therefore help considerably in casting a design that will be appropriate. However, such a person is not the ultimate end-user client, that is, the person who owns the problem and is seeking to solve it with some research – and obviously it is important that the end-user is familiar with and happy with the design. As will be described later, this simple fact is often much harder to achieve than would at first appear.

In addition, the 'client' could actually be this ultimate end-user and be dealing directly with the outside researcher. This client may be very experienced and have realistic expectations of the research, in terms of cost, timing and utility. He or she may be working with researchers with whom he or she has worked for years, so that considerable trust has grown up between them. Alternatively, such an end-user may be very naive, with unrealistic expectations, and have considerable difficulty in couching the problems in a way that is amenable to research.

Depending upon the nature of the client, the balance of involvement in the design will vary. In the case where this is an in-house researcher, the design may effectively be done internally and confirmed or 'tweaked' by the outside researcher. Provided this is done with proper respect accorded to the feelings and experience of the outside researcher, this is in many ways a good system, as it removes from the outside researcher a number of often intractable problems like understanding the political context of the research. However, not all in-house researchers are comfortable with doing this, and they may talk with the outside researcher before any design is created, so the design is built up through mutual discussion. In both these cases the in-house researcher should in the end take the responsibility for the design being an appropriate one that will deliver the goods. Sometimes, however, life is not fair!

An alternative approach is for the company to specify the nature of the problem in general terms, send it to a number of researchers or agencies and invite them to make proposals to solve it. In this case, the company may well be looking for imaginative solutions to be offered, and could be choosing using this criterion rather than cost. Sometimes the client has decided upon a general approach, for example, 'accompanied shopping', 'semiotics', conjoint and so on, and therefore limits the agencies or researchers it approaches to those it rightly or wrongly believes have skill and experience in this chosen area of investigation. Reasons for selecting particular researchers or agencies were given in some detail in Chapter 5.

THE COMPONENTS OF A DESIGN OF RESEARCH

In purely logical terms, it is proper that the method to be used is decided last, as it is only after working out what is going to be addressed and among whom that it makes any sense at all to decide upon the method. The reason that the logical approach is often not followed will be addressed later in this chapter.

The main elements of a research design will now be taken in turn, but it must be said in advance that the biggest issue of all is correctly identifying the problem that is to be addressed, and the reasons for this difficulty will be discussed in detail.

Problem definition

The single most critical feature of a research design is to discover what the problem is – a better brief means better research (Pyke, 2000). Only in this way may the research be reduced to a series of objectives – or desired outcomes – around which the research may be designed.

In many ways it seems absurd to state that the setting of the objectives is so critical, but the fact that there is confusion over why the research is being done is the major reason for research failing. When the client believes one thing and the researcher another, then this is clearly a recipe for disaster and disappointment. So why can this happen?

The problem holder often does not know what the problem is

On the whole, marketing people are not very good at expressing the problem in researchable ways (they tend to be 'doing' people in line with the mainstream of business employees), and it is necessary almost to interview them in depth to find out what the problem really is, and to get it couched in terms that are amenable to research.

For example, a brand manager has the idea that it would be 'good' to create a new variant of the brand and wants to know the scale of the opportunity for it. From this, the impact on production and the possible magnitude of the advertising spend can be assessed. This would suggest some form of quantitative concept test. But what exactly is the variant to be? How does it fit with other things that are happening on the market? Is the brand able to credibly stretch to encompass the variant? There are many questions like this that are obviously the meat of qualitative research, and their answers could radically colour the decision whether to make the variant at all. The discussion with the brand manager might miss out entirely worries that others in the company have, because he or she is too focused.

The market assumptions radically affect the design

Another typical problem could be that 'We are selling less of this stuff and want to do some research to find out why so that we know how to sell more.' There are fairly obvious possible causes for this, which are very easy to brainstorm. For example, is it price, distribution, competitor activity, the product proposition, the market and so on? To address all the potential reasons for the problem existing would require a very large-scale and probably multi-staged approach, which would be very expensive, take too much time, and is in fact generally not necessary.

The client will have some ideas about what the problem is, and these ideas can be used to reduce the scale of the research. Therefore, in the briefing meeting there is a need to identify as much as possible what the hypotheses of the organization are as to the poor performance of the product, and to use these in creating the design.

The researcher will attempt to find these out through talking to the client, and in doing so will sometimes have to use all his or her skill as an interviewer. Often this can become a process of negotiation, and has as much to do with the client and his or her experience (or its lack) as it does with the problem.

In this process lies a deep problem, in that the assumptions being taken into the research can radically impact on the outcome. If a given area is not deemed to be important, and is therefore not addressed in the research design, then the research will obviously not uncover it – even if it were to be the critical factor. There are some who believe that the need to produce 'efficient' designs is strongly distorting the use of the research in that the outcome effectively becomes ordained (Gordon, 1999).

So getting the balance right about the assumptions is important, and worthy of challenging. It is also sensible to include the assumptions that are being worked on in the research design documentation, so that over the course of time it is apparent why a particular subgroup or area of investigation (which with the benefit of hindsight was clearly of importance) was excluded from that particular piece of research.

Different clients see the world differently

The intrinsic ambiguity of problem definition is made worse because different people may see the problem in a different way. Typically this could be within the organization's hierarchy, when it is clear whose opinion counts most, but it can also be the case that a problem has a number of different stakeholders (see Chapter 1): for example, the advertising agency may have a different view from the manufacturing client for whom it works.

In the example given earlier in this section about the new variant, there may be those in the company who are concerned about the possible cannibalization of the current brand by its variant, with no real increase in sales but at greater costs associated with managing two variants rather than one. Knowing that this is a concern of one of the stakeholders could put a very different spin on the resulting design.

This means that a briefing given by one person will often lead to a different view about the 'problem' and lead to a different research design than would have been the case had the briefing come from another person in the same organization.

A junior does the briefing

A common situation is that the client who is briefing the researcher is actually not the problem holder but is a junior who has been told to 'go and get some research'. Under these circumstances the real problem holder does not have direct contact with the researcher, and there may be multiple links in the chain, with an abundant opportunity for the message to get confused and weakened. The junior manager probably thinks he or she understands the problem, might also have his or her own ideas (which may or may not be helpful) and may be quite forceful about this (marketing people are like that!), so it is very difficult for the researcher, when presented with such a person, to appreciate exactly how ignorant of the problem he or she really is.

An example of this was when a chief executive of a company, which was in the process of buying a major retail chain in the United States, speculated out loud about the relative consumer awareness of the competing chains. Within a day this was translated into a research request to conduct an awareness study in every state in the United States. This was said to have had the backing of the chief executive, and therefore by implication, money was no object. Fortunately, in this case the request did not go directly to a research agency. If it had, it would have been quite impossible for it to have discovered that the chief executive in question had no recollection of even thinking about awareness, let alone asking for some research on it. In this case the request had gone to the internal research department, which was able to find out the truth. The role of the internal research department has been discussed in some detail in Chapter 4.

Remote briefing

Since getting to the problem can be very difficult at the best of times, there is clearly a major problem when the client is unprepared to spend time with the researcher to go through these preliminary stages. Unfortunately this is not uncommon, and it is not that unusual for a brief to arrive in the form of a two-line fax: for example, 'some groups are needed on a new packaging'! After this the client becomes impossible to contact, never being available and never returning calls. In-house researchers who are preparing a briefing for an outside qualitative researcher may be briefed on the way to lunch, at the end of a meeting on another topic or by similar limited communications. It is under these circumstances that continuity of supply becomes a great advantage, either between the in-house researcher and his or her internal end-user clients, or though the direct relationship that a researcher builds up with the end-user, so that it is possible to develop some approximation to the telepathic skills needed to deal with clients like this.

The situation changes by magic

Telepathic skills are very useful to a researcher when dealing with a client. Once a brief has been received and the best possible attempt had been made at getting it into an agreed form, in terms of setting the research objectives, it is possible that it will change. Such is the way of the world, that it is not uncommon for the researcher to be expected to know this by telepathy. This happens as much between internal researchers and their internal clients as it does for direct researcher–end-user relationships, and there is really not much that can be done about it other than to cope as best as possible when the changes are discovered – which could actually be in the debrief! So it really is important for there to be constant communication between the client and the agency.

The sample definition

One of the most important features of a research design is the definition of the sample of respondents to be used. It goes without saying that the information collected will depend upon the experience and orientation of the people being questioned.

The whole issue of the sample relates to the concept of the research *franchise* developed in Chapter 1, which in turn relates to the varying perspectives of the research stakeholders. Consequently, the broad definition of the extent of the sample (or more correctly, samples) derives directly from the research objectives as viewed by different stakeholders. Once this has been decided on, there is then a need to specify in more detail the *nature* of the various samples. This is done in completely different ways for quantitative research and qualitative research.

In quantitative research, the sample needs to be specified in such a way that the people questioned are *representative* of something – possibly the population in general (as is the case in most omnibus work) or the participants in some 'market' or other (if we take a broad definition as to what a 'market' is). 'Representativeness' is important to quantitative researchers who are counting responses, and is a major way of achieving reliability (that is, repeatability). Representativeness means not only that the right people should be in the sample, but that *they should be there in the right proportions*, or if not, the deviation from this proportion should be known so that corrections can be applied later at the analysis stage. So far this is easy to understand, but it is not so easy in the case of qualitative research.

In qualitative research there is no need for the sample to be constructed in this way, and in general this would be entirely counter-productive. The need is to have representatives of *different views* present so that these can be understood and taken into account. Many products that are the subject of qualitative research are mass-market products, and there is a tendency to spread the constituents of the sample through the demographic, regional and possibly usage base of the market. However, it is very rare that the differences between these people are sufficiently great to merit separate reporting, and their presence simply helps to add to the overall richness of the information being collected. The qualitative researcher's job therefore becomes one of putting together the story from the many fragments with which he or she is presented by the individual respondents. It should never be forgotten that much of what is researched is not something that people have spent much time, or any time for that matter, articulating themselves, so it is unlikely that anyone will have the whole story.

However, this situation is not always the case, and the structure of the sample can become an important part of the data collection itself. A common divide is to compare users with lapsed users, in terms of what type of people they are, their relationship to the market and the needs that they are seeking to be addressed. Alternatively, one might want to look at committed users of different brands in the market in order to understand the *brand positions* better, or select people who use the product in a different way, in order to examine the *needs* in the market. Occasionally one might want to counterpoint the views of people who express a different attitude to the products or the market, for example, those who are price sensitive as opposed to those who are not.

When a sample is constructed in this way, then the sample design is absolutely critical to the planned method of analysis, and possibly even the reporting of the results. This is an example of the 'all at oneness' of qualitative research, where all aspects of it seem to be coincident.

The use of the term 'representative' therefore becomes quite different when applied to qualitative research or to quantitative research, and when used in a survey it should be considered in terms of the specified sample design, not of the market in general.

Sample size

In quantitative research, the sample size is supposed to be determined by the statistical significance of any difference that it is hoped will be discovered. A given numerical difference can be attributed a 'significance', that is, the probability of it being 'true' (or more properly, the 'null' hypotheses being false), and this depends upon the variation in the base data and the number of measures of it (that is, respondents). Consequently, the sample size should be selected against assumptions about these two expectations. In reality sample sizes are rarely arrived at in this way, and are more to do with the credibility associated with the size of any subsamples that will be analysed and the cost of the research.

The way that the numbers of interviews are worked out for a qualitative sample does have a parallel to that of a quantitative survey, but not much. The issue at stake is how similar the views of the respondents are to the main issues. If they speak with one voice, then in all practical respects one only needs to talk to one of them to have all the information. If the segmentation of views is categorical, for example all brand users say one thing and non-brand users say another, then again in principle, only one respondent from each category would be needed – as *good quality findings* would be obtained in such a hypothetical case as if a thousand people had been interviewed (see Chapter 5).

Of course, the majority of topics that are subjected to commercial qualitative research are not burning issues in the minds of the respondents, and help is needed to get them to articulate 'good stuff'. However, even under the most skilled interviewing, in most cases it seems that only bits of the picture emerge from the various interviewees and it is from these bits that the whole must be synthesized. Consequently, even under these circumstances, it is necessary to have a range of people. Sometimes, if the researcher is lucky, there will be one person among them who enables the researcher to make sense of all these pieces and allow the jigsaw to be put together.

Sample size and sample segmentation go hand in hand in the qualitative research designs for good reasons. Not only does a quality and sensible segmentation of respondents help with obtaining a clear analysis – because different views become concentrated into different groups – but also it can actually reduce the total number of respondents needed because of this greater clarity. In the quantitative case, segmentation always increases the numbers of respondents needed, as they need to be identified in a sub-break at credible analytical numbers.

Coverage

A fairly obvious part of the research design is the questions to be asked. However, the notion of 'question' is very much one that comes from the quantitative research paradigm, so I am using the term '*coverage*' as a more general term applicable to both quantitative and qualitative research.

Clients tend only to think about 'questions' and 'issues' and are inclined to confuse *the business* questions that are to be answered by the research with *the actual* questions that are to be asked to get the information required from the respondents.

Obviously, a number of business questions *can* be answered by directly asking the respondent. 'What don't you like about this product?' is an example. But other business questions, especially those related to the question 'Why?' – essentially motivations and needs – cannot be understood by direct questions. Consequently, indirect approaches need to be adopted.

In the case of quantitative research, questions need to be put together so that an analysis can be done. Often this involves questions that enable the respondent to be characterized in a way that is helpful to the analysis. The most obvious of these is demographics. But there are generally more powerful ways of contrasting respondent views and thereby gaining insight. For example, usage and other behavioural questions, although having obvious direct applicability, are very powerful at doing this. An example relevant to the leisure market is that *who* the respondents are *with* will have an effect on what sort of things that they *do* – a group of girls on a night out is different from a group of boys, and both are different when they mix. A considerable part of the skill in achieving a good quantitative analysis is in identifying the questions to be used to segment the sample.

Mathematical techniques can be used to extract information from the respondents. Examples of these are trade-off or multivariate methods that impute levels of importance – so-called 'latent methods' – and these require particular schemes of questioning, the use of which may not be obviously apparent to the client. Generally speaking, clients are not good at understanding why questions of this type (that are present to enable analysis rather than directly generate information that has obvious utility) are included, and it may require some debate before they allow their inclusion.

As already mentioned, the notion of *'question'* does not have much meaning in qualitative research, in that questions, such that they occur, are generally aimed at getting the respondents to start talking, and thereby start revealing their relationship to the topic in hand. Normally the coverage of qualitative research is communicated through the medium of the 'interview guide'. This is really a loose plan of action, and lays out which particular areas will be explored, in which order and in what way. These areas are themselves selected as being appropriate in order to elicit information that will help towards achieving the objectives of the research – that is, answer the client's questions. Qualitative researchers will often use some form of enabling or projective technique with their respondents to help them access and express their thoughts. This is not intended to *deceive* the respondents, but to help them marshal their thoughts in order to allow them to give information on a topic they will normally have thought very little about.

Methodology

This book is not about methodology, there are many others on this topic, but given the all-important qualitative/quantitative divide it is necessary to understand how this choice is made for any particular design.

Although the decision about methodology logically should take place after the aim, purpose and objectives of the research are known, in practice it tends to be the first question requiring an answer. Not only does this influence which suppliers one might turn to, but it also affects the time span.

The standard 'textbook' solution as to which is the preferred method in any particular case is to say that quantitative research has value when one is interested in the sizes of markets or the numbers of people interested in something, and that qualitative research is of value when one wants to understand people's relationship to the issue. But this is to trivialize the complexity of the real factors that determine the choice of method. Broadly speaking, these are the requirements as to the timing of the research and the context and politics of the environment in which the results are to be used.

The next two sections deal with the *practical* reasons for selecting a particular research methodology even though it may strictly be inappropriate, and are followed by two further sections explaining the actual strengths and weaknesses of the qualitative and quantitative methods.

Some arguments need quantitative data to be politically effective

Sometimes arguments need to be supported with numbers to have any credibility (see Chapters 6 and 7), and in this case it is only sensible to use quantitative research because it will better enable the decision than using (possibly more correct) qualitative research.

These circumstances can arise because a particular individual who is critical to the decision feels more comfortable with quantitative data, and feels he or she can more easily defend his or her position by using it. Alternatively, a decision may be made by a board, and it will involve a large financial commitment. Under these circumstances, especially when the board includes a number of non-marketing specialists, it is most unlikely to respond to arguments that are only supported qualitatively. Another case can be when one company is talking to another.

If either of these companies is particularly numbers oriented, quantitative data will be needed irrespective of its relevance. Typically, American companies are even more number driven than those in the United Kingdom.

Short turnaround timings favour qualitative research

On the whole, it is possible to turn qualitative research round more quickly than quantitative research, and it is not uncommon for qualitative research to be the preferred methodology for this reason alone, even though it is clearly not the correct methodology.

There are some interesting ethical issues to this. Is it right to accept a job which should be quantitative but where time pressures impose a requirement for it to be qualitative? The industry is mixed in the answer to this type of ethical question (Lovett, 2001). On one hand, these types of requests often arrive in the context of long-established relationships, and become difficult (or financially dangerous) not to accept. On the other hand, within a long-term relationship it is unlikely that the research would be wholly wasted. More knowledge of the topic would be produced and this would be generally advantageous. These arguments tend to be a bit of a moral cop-out, but we are all human after all! The question researchers tend to ask themselves is whether doing the research, even in the wrong methodological form, actually benefits the company or not, and the answer is often that it does. In the absence of the 'proper stuff' a substitute can be better than nothing, and in this case it seems reasonable to feel that it is not wrong to do it, just that it would have been more efficient to do it in the alternative way given the time.

Real reasons for preferring quantitative research

As was mentioned earlier in this book, quantitative research has not been able to address the deeper relational-type questions that have emerged as the ideas around branding have become more developed, and in part this explained why qualitative research has grown up in an environment that is generally attitudinally hostile to it. However, there are signs that quantitative research may be moving into a new gear, and this is because of the increasing awareness of the amount of internally generated quantitative data businesses now have, and the increasing consciousness that some use should be made of it.

There is another reason that quantitative research may be undergoing a revival, and this is due to the ability to create mathematical models from data and give them to clients in the form of spreadsheets to do their own 'what ifs' with. This has, of course, been possible for many years, but the increasing familiarity with spreadsheets is a facilitating agent. Particular areas where this is of great interest are volume estimations, price–brand trade-off and concept development based on conjoint models.

In addition, the opportunities of calibrating internal data by joining it, or a sample of it, to quantitative market research are opening up many new ways in which market research can contribute to the company's knowledge. As was mentioned in Chapter 6, this could mean there will be a renaissance in the use of quantitative research, which could be termed the *'new quantitative'*.

So for these two different reasons, it seems likely that quantitative research is about to receive an added boost, especially in companies that have created consumer insight departments.

Real reasons for preferring qualitative research

Qualitative research is used whenever a relationship between a 'consumer' and an 'object' is to be understood and explored. Chapter 7 examined the nature of qualitative information compared with quantitative information, and the earlier sections of this chapter explored why the methodology that is logically 'correct' is not always the one that is used.

The qualitative task may be exploratory in nature or part of a linked multi-stage programme of work (see Chapter 10), but normally it is rare that any client really wants to do either of these things; clients want to know what to do, and to have the evidence that helps them achieve this. Furthermore, they want to know it now! Consequently, qualitative research is more likely to be used to address a straightforward tactical decision relating to the everyday matters of marketing. Such problems are generally amenable to direct solution, and often the decision can be made in the debrief itself.

Tactical qualitative problems come in a variety of forms, and it can be convenient to think of them as loosely falling into four categories: those related to a product, those related to an expression of a product, those related to a brand and those related to advertising.

The 'product' is an object that has characteristics that need to be defined and understood, generally for the purpose of subsequently manipulating them to improve its appeal. Taking this definition, products come in many forms, for example, a chocolate bar, the layout of a building society outlet, the nature of customer service delivery for a utility supplier, the way a company employee benefits package is put together or the nature of the company culture itself can all be viewed as being the 'product'.

Sometimes it is worth thinking in terms of the *expression* of the product, for example the pack, a restaurant menu, a description of a financial service or a political party's policy. The expression is not only the product, which clearly predicates it, but also includes a communication dimension as well; indeed it may be wholly communicational in nature. Research into a product expression is generally about ensuring that someone approaching it can easily deduce its relevant properties.

Work put into a brand is fundamentally about the *position* (which necessarily includes the market structure) and its development or extension. However, it is not unusual for product and product expression work to be seen as part of brand work – which in some ways it is.

Research into advertising is mostly very closely linked to the brand itself. There are some people who think that the advertising is the brand, although others would disagree, saying that the brand is more about the accumulated experiences that people have had with it rather than simply one contact with one advertising campaign. Advertising itself is also not only about brand matters. Companies can use advertising to make simple announcements about promotions or sales or some other such thing. Much government advertising is about public information, for example the need to get tax forms in by a certain date, or the availability of some benefit. In this case, this government advertising is like a *product expression* – does it get over the message about the important elements of the product (in this case the taxation system)? Alternatively, government advertising may be about changing public attitudes, for example to drugs or alcohol. In this latter case, the need for the advertising to change behaviour with respect to a product field (in this case drugs/alcohol) is nearer the objectives of brand advertising, though not quite the same.

Clearly, these are topics where qualitative research is able to illuminate in a way that quantitative research cannot.

Stimulus material

Before this chapter on the design of research ends, it is important not to forget the role of stimulus material – because it *is* so often forgotten. One of the reasons for this is that generally stimulus material is the province of another agency. It could be from the advertising agency, a brand consultancy or from the technical department. Stimulus material is something that is given to respondents for them to see, handle, feel, touch, consume, examine and experience, and is a way of getting them into a more concrete frame of mind. Sometimes the stimulus material is the sole reason for the research, as for example is the case in product or concept testing. At other times it is an adjunct to help the respondent conceptualize something through, say, the medium of a mood board.

It is surprising how often stimulus material causes problems. Even with such simple things as a product test, one has to be sure that the products used are properly representative of the products available, or at the very least, properly characterized. The products used may not be what one expected. For example, there are batch-to-batch variations in manufacture, and these may be big enough to influence the results. If a formulation change is being tested, it is normal for the new formula to be quite close to the old one, and it may therefore be essential to test it against a current batch of product that is exactly on specification, rather than within specification. Another problem that can occur with product testing is the mixing up of product codes. This is surprisingly easy to do, and when this happens we never really know.

The 'stimulus material' could be a product 'experience' such as telling respondents to go and shop at a particular store. This experience could be different depending upon the time of day or week they did it, who they were with, and what they actually bought. If these extraneous factors do have an impact on the experience then they should be specified to respondents, or at the very minimum captured on the questionnaire so that their impact can be examined at the analysis stage.

Another form of 'product' is a 'new product concept'. These are very difficult to communicate – if only because of their newness – and this simple and obvious fact is hardly ever properly addressed. Great care should be applied in the construction of stimulus material of this type, and it should really be the topic of a number of meetings because it is the linchpin upon which the research is based. Unfortunately, it is much more common for the stimulus material to *never have been seen* by the end-user client before it goes into research.

A further issue with stimulus material is the simple logistics of getting it into the right place at the right time, and it is not that infrequent that the timings involved in getting stimulus material prepared become the factors that determine the timing of the whole research. Furthermore, the stimulus material might get damaged in transport, for example, the chocolate bars being tested might get heated and slightly melt, and this type of damage is all the more insidious for not being known.

In qualitative research all the above applies, but in general the issue is more under control, as at least the moderator can detect if something has gone wrong. Many qualitative researchers feel that they cannot have too much stimulus material from which to choose, and consequently the nature of stimulus material tends to be more diverse in qualitative research than quantitative research. As with quantitative research, stimulus material can take the form of a product, a pack or advertising, but is very likely to also include mood boards, sets of words, photographs of people, and possibly the place in which the interviewing is taking place (such as a retail environment). The problems with researching fully finished adverts are legion, and the difficulties of doing it with some form of representation of it are extraordinary.

Another way of stimulating people within the qualitative environment is to put them through a series of enabling or projective techniques (which are generally not used in quantitative research), the objective of which is to get respondents to be more lucid. It is also not unreasonable to think of the members of the group as being, in part, 'stimulus material' as they *do* stimulate each other and may be particularly chosen to do so.

In summary, stimulus material provides an area where many things can go wrong, and its inclusion in the actual design helps to concentrate the mind and reduce the likelihood of this happening.

WHO HAS A STAKE IN THE DESIGN

In the first part of this chapter, it was pointed out that the design is negotiated between the research supplier and a research user, and clearly these are the two primary stakeholders in the design. In addition there are others who have an important stake in the design; these are the rest of the research stakeholders (as described in Chapter 1). The importance of capturing the opinions and wishes of this diverse group cannot be overestimated.

Apart from those interested in the *output* of the research, there is also a group of people that have an interest in the *process* of the research and they should also be considered at the design stage. Unfortunately the needs of these people are frequently ignored, which can be detrimental to the research itself, either because the quality is prejudiced or because it becomes more expensive to do, or both.

Perhaps most important are the respondents themselves and the recruiters and interviewers who have to face them, and to be fair their needs are generally given some passing thought. But there are others who work in the depths of the research agency whose interests and needs are mostly neglected. This is unfortunate and unfair, as is the best work of anybody going to be done at midnight? There are also the requirements and the reality of the legal framework in which the research is done, particularly data and privacy legislation, and the professional environment as embodied in the Code of Conduct of the Market Research Society.

We will now consider in more detail those who are affected by the chosen research processes.

The respondents

The *respondents* should obviously be respected and not placed in embarrassing situations, and thought should be given to what they will be expected to do and the practical implications of this. This involves being sensitive to the nature of questions or the questioning areas that they will be put through, the time that it might take and the level of interest that the research experience will invoke. Good data does not come from bored, embarrassed or stressed respondents. There is also the general appropriateness of thinking about the 'market' of respondents for the future. Already response rates are falling dramatically and there is no need to wilfully accelerate this process.

In terms of qualitative research, not loading clients into the room to observe the respondents like animals in a zoo, or having people laughing at them from behind mirrors is not only polite, but also helps generate better information. Similarly, if the respondents are expected to eat (sample a product, for example), they need to be forewarned (so that they can reduce the amount they eat beforehand if necessary), or if they will be expected to read they may need to know this in order to bring their glasses (Imms, 2001).

The recruiter

The *recruiter's* needs vary, depending upon whether he or she is recruiting for qualitative or quantitative work. In general, in quantitative recruitment the recruiter is also the interviewer, whereas in the case of qualitative research this is rarely the case. Quantitative recruitment is about finding people to interview on the spot, typically using quota controls, although occasionally there is a requirement to recruit people against a pre-selected list. Examples of this are addresses selected by a random method or from customer lists; sometimes there is a need to pre-recruit people for a later purpose.

To meet the sample requirements, the recruiter needs the research design to be as flexible as possible. For example, quotas can be made interlocking, which means that specific combinations of recruitment criteria are needed, such as men and women of specific age bands. Having such quotas dramatically increases the recruitment task (and therefore directly increases the cost of fieldwork) and so they should only be required when this really adds to the design. Similarly, *time of day* of interview may be specified, which often implies a time of day for recruitment. But ease of recruitment can vary greatly across the time of day. For example, recruitment of many groups by door-knocking is difficult during the day as people simply are not at home, while recruitment at night is difficult because many people are reluctant to open the door. In addition, the *geographical area* of recruitment needs to be considered, as there are places in a town to which recruiters (and many other people too!) will not want to go. Furthermore, the *physical characteristics* of the place of recruitment need to be considered carefully. For example, recruitment and interview may be required in a retail outlet. This is much easier if there is a lot of space, and more difficult if the place is small or very crowded, where the interviewer may get in the way of the operation of the outlet. Recruitment in nightclubs can present its own problems due to the noise.

In the case of qualitative recruitment, if groups are specified, there must be a sufficient concentration of potential respondents in a geographical area. Otherwise, expensive 'bussing' of respondents will be needed. If there is not a concentration, perhaps alternatives ways of doing the research should be considered – by depth interview for example, or by using one of the newer online methods. It is important that what *is* to be recruited is as closely defined as possible, but that the 'spirit' of the required respondents is also appreciated. For example, it may be important to separate out who did the *buying* from those who influenced the *purchase choice,* and possibly from those who did the *consuming.* They could all be the same people, or they could all be different. Tightly defined demographics may still produce a range of attitudinally disparate people due to life-stage difference, for example a 25-year-old mother as opposed to a 25-year-old single person. Also, what on the face of it might seem to be a clear specification of a person's *category* – for example 'student' – may produce people who are different from a classic university undergraduate. A recruiter also needs enough time to do the job properly, and in general this time period should include at least two weekends if a well-recruited sample is to be achieved.

Of course, the difficulties of recruitment are as numerous as there are possible research designs, and the message here is that the issue of recruitment should be considered at the design stage. The design should, if possible, take into account the complications of the recruitment process and try to make it as easy as possible.

The interviewer/moderator

In general, the interviewer's difficulties are largely ones of recruitment prior to the interview taking place, but the actual process of the interview can be made either more or less difficult. Putting aside the aspect of making the questionnaire interesting and relevant to the respondent, there are also practical considerations to take into account. If the questionnaire is to be done without the aid of computers, then the routing and layout of the questionnaire needs to be considered carefully, as if this is badly done the interviewer will make mistakes when going though the questionnaire, which is of no help to anyone. Also, the use of prompting cards has to be thought out properly, as the interviewer may be in a situation of having to handle multiple cards, asking the questions and recording the answers in the correct boxes all at the same time. A little thought can often save a lot of trouble. Other stimulus material also needs to be thought about: are the photographs unwieldy? Is any product that may be placed in front of respondents easily transported by the interviewer? and so forth. Many of the problems that interviewers face can be radically reduced by a little sympathetic care at the design stage – and thinking about these things means that the research is often cheaper and the research agency can more easily get interviewers to take on the job.

In qualitative research, the moderator normally has direct contact with the client and can generally easily get his or her personal perspective fed into the design. Among the most obvious requirement is that the group needs to be constructed so that the people will be happy to talk with one another. This means that care has to be taken about mixing sexes (especially with older women), age differences (especially with teenagers) and class differences. Also the environment of the discussion has to be considered, as well as the requirements of stimulus material (considered earlier in the chapter).

Production departments

The various groups that comprise agency 'production' hardly ever receive the attention at the design stage that they ought to. These groups include: printing and dispatch, field department, data preparation and the data processing department. In general, the activities of these departments occur in a sequence, one after the other, so that problems at any one stage become timing problems at the next. For this reason, it is of great help if they can have as much information in advance as possible.

The primary problem for these groups is lateness, and it is particularly pernicious. It introduces the chance of error as well as making the staff that work in these departments unnecessarily stressed. For example, leaving approval of the questionnaire to the end of the day may mean that it is has to be printed overnight, with all the possibilities of error that this is likely to introduce. Similarly, the field department needs to get the recruiters and interviewers (who need to be properly trained and supervised), brief them about the job, get the materials to them that they need, and, if necessary, book halls and arrange for them to be equipped appropriately for the research to take place. All this takes time, and the more time there is to do it (in principle) the better the job that can be done. The data processing department comes into play right at the final stages of the production process, and it is they that tends to have ultimately to pick up any shortfalls in time.

It is helpful to provide the table specification ahead of the data, and not too many post-tabulation requests should be made since they become disruptive to subsequent jobs.

Summary of the various perspectives on research design

Some of the above issues may seem not of much concern to a client-side researcher, and to a great extent they are not. These are the matters for the research agency. However, the agency is often in the position of having difficulties in this area, because the client has set up a series of requirements at the design stage without thinking at all about the impact of what is being asked. In the end the client will get what he or she asks for, but it is a sensible client who realizes how requests can adversely impact on data quality, cost and the attitudes of the many people who have to implement what may be unnecessarily difficult requirements.

CONCLUSION

The research design is critical in the process of ensuring that end-user clients get the results they need. Within the design elements, the most important one is getting the research objectives correct. This is much more difficult than it would at first seem, due to the diversity of stake-holders who may be interested in the outcome and the difficulty of discovering who they are. If the research objectives are right then the professionalism of the industry takes over, and a good result is likely. Consideration of the various aspects discussed in this chapter will load the dice in favour of this happening.

9 Managing the research process from within the company

This chapter brings together material from Chapters 4 and 8 into the whole means of managing the research process from the perspective of the commissioner. The early stages of the research process are a bit confusing because of the overlap in the stages of creating a design and of selecting a researcher, plus the further complication of the occasional need for competitive bidding. These vary greatly from organization to organization and also from job to job. The later stages are easier to describe, as they are more likely to occur in a logical and common sequence. These are the stages that take place after the 'button has been pushed' when the research is commissioned, and cover such aspects as contact during the fieldwork and analysis period, preparation for the debrief, the debrief itself, and after the debrief.

KEY POINTS

- Every large organization has some form of process for the commissioning of research. These processes are quite difficult to keep in place because of pressures not to follow them – some reasons are legitimate and some not.
- The initial elements of the process are: to be able to recognize that research is required and to enter a preliminary process in which a research specification is agreed. This may involve the job being effectively designed in the client company, or a design selected from a competitive pitch, or all stations in between.
- It is desirable that as many people as possible are party to this process so that they can have an input. This helps to increase the chances that the purpose and objectives are appropriate and that the assumptions built into the design are acceptable to all the stakeholders.
- Once the design has been agreed (the way this is done varies between companies and jobs), the job has to be managed through fieldwork to debrief. Although the majority of this work is in the hands of the external researcher or agencies, there are a number of things that the internal buyer can do to help the process. These include ensuring that the researcher has all the things he or she needs on time, has access to the buyer, and that the end-user clients' relationship with the research is managed.
- It is especially important that the researcher or agency is not put under pressure to come to preliminary conclusions before it has finished its analysis, especially when the research is qualitative.
- The debrief needs to be managed carefully so that the end-user clients do not end up being unprepared for being presented with controversial findings. The researcher needs to be informed of the social and political dynamics of the groups that will attend the debrief, and also proper attention should be paid to the facilities available to him/her to undertake the debrief.

HAVING SOME FORM OF PROCESS

In general, organizations that commission a lot of research have a process for commissioning it, which is accepted and sort of followed.

However this does not mean that it is a good process; in fact it might be terrible. The research function should constantly be trying to maintain the presence of a resemblance to a formal process, and of course, trying to improve it. Much depends upon the status of the research function within the organization as to how effective it is at this (see Chapter 4).

Although it is fairly obvious that some sort of process should be defined, it is in fact surprisingly difficult to do, as there are many forces that work against it. The forces that stop the smooth commissioning of research are basically twofold and relate to the way marketing people organize themselves and the fact that information is power.

It does seem that marketing people on the whole seem to take on too much work, and their world appears to be one of chaos. The whole marketing services industry that serves them appears to be constructed to accommodate this. Within this environment work gets commissioned very late, and to achieve the imposed deadlines means that it is difficult to follow a set process. This is a matter of fact, and therefore the processes have to be able to accommodate it.

A more pernicious fact is that information is power, and any process that is channelling power may be doing so in a way that others may not wish. For example, there may be many reasons why a particular person in an organization does not want a piece of research to take place, and would be happy to see it fail as a result of some process failure, if he or she can engineer it. The research manager needs to be sensitive to these problems and to lay torpedo nets to catch any torpedoes that may be aimed at a project which otherwise will come out of the blue with a possibly devastating effect.

A major problem with any process is that there will always be occasions when it really does get in the way of acting sensibly, and it is on these occasions that evidence can be built up to be used against it. It is therefore prudent that whatever the process, it can be adapted and is flexible.

THE ELEMENTS OF A PROCESS

The elements of a process are, first, the initial stages and the genesis of the research, leading to the research specification; second, managing the research through the field to the point of an analysis being achieved;

and third, the handling of the information transfer from the researcher to the end-user. Of these three stages, it is the first (getting to the research specification) that is most difficult to define. The second two stages are clearer and tend to follow a consistent course.

THE INITIAL STAGES: THE GENESIS OF THE RESEARCH

Capturing the fact that research is needed and aspects of its nature

In general, the need for market research is likely to appear quite late on in the development of a marketing project. This is because it will not have been fully planned, or because the need for it was genuinely not anticipated. The research manager can become aware of the need for research in a variety of informal ways. Examples include reading it in the minutes of a meeting he or she was not present at, hearing it mentioned by an outside agency (for example the advertising agency), being dropped a few lines of e-mail or a memo, and having it said in passing in the corridor on the way to lunch. Lucky research managers may hear of it through a formal meeting being set up to discuss it.

Whatever the method, a meeting has to be arranged so that the essential facts can be captured. This really means the time the results are wanted, who needs to be involved in the discussions, and a reasonable conversation about the issues to be researched. Naturally, within companies that are continuously commissioning research, the research manager will know a great deal of the background for much of the research that is being commissioned, and this can short-circuit a lot of the debate. It is, however, really important to get to grips with the particular aspects of a job (including any politics – which are often benign).

Finally, it is necessary to identify any relevant logistical matters, such as the availability of product, contact lists or stimulus material or the need to get permissions, for example, from an operator to get access to its premises or people. Although these seem unimportant in comparison with the previously mentioned matters, they are generally determining factors in the whole project and need to be started as soon as possible.

Given that the research manager has obtained this information, he or she is in a position to identify any critical points on the timing path and to start working on them right away. Generally this means checking the availability of the research supplier and pressing some of the buttons on logistic matters.

Preliminary documentation and awareness that the research may happen

Following on from establishing that research is required, a document needs to be created laying out the dimensions of the research. This normally includes some background, probably the general nature, scope and scale of the research, some thoughts about the budget that is required, and the timings (which are often critical and short). This document may be circulated among the interested parties for comment, and also in order to raise a consciousness that the research is happening. In some cases it is possible to discover at this stage that non-research information already exists on the research topic, and that in this light, the research is not necessary at all. It is important that the research that is proposed is seen to be that of the company, not of the individual, and that people within the company or its agencies feel able and empowered to make critical comments about it. The document may also form the basis for briefing a research agency. On the other hand this document might be created by the agency if it has been involved at this point. This is one of the variations in process that can occur.

It is very important to circulate the research document as widely as possible, as this aspect of the process is all about ensuring that the ultimate design is going to work, that nothing of importance has been left out and that torpedoes (if any) can be dealt with harmlessly. However, it is still important that there is only one internal commissioning client, who ultimately takes the responsibility of agreeing the objectives of the research and the timings of it.

Creation of the research design

Chapter 8 described the basic elements of a research design, and showed that an important aspect of this is to take on board the market assumptions and hypotheses held within the company, as this is a way to simplify the research and constrain its costs. This could be achieved by including a draft design within the initial circulated document, although, of course, the design might not have been originated at that point.

The design may be done in the commissioning company to a fairly defined state, or a briefing document may go out to tender among an appropriate set of potential suppliers (which may only be one) selected according to the principles described in Chapter 5. As described, in practice there are a number of ways this can be done, depending upon the complexity of the job and the level of process that the company normally requires. At the most informal end of the spectrum, a single research supplier may be briefed by phone (although it is generally better to have a face-to-face meeting), and the agency asked to produce a response in the form of a proposal (which may be either an outline or detailed), and this proposal may be the actual paper that is internally circulated. At the briefing of the agency, the internal end-user may or may not be present. This will depend on what the end-user wants – often how interested he or she is in the outcome of the project, or simply the level of his or her interest in research.

Whatever is created as a result of this process is likely to be subject to some alteration, and the proposal will be honed. Once again this may be a long and detailed process, or it could simply be that the initial proposal is accepted in totality.

The research specification

The changes to the initial research proposal will arise from a series of inputs that have been made as a result of discussions with the supplier, or from comments arising from the circulation of the initial documents. These changes could involve the sample that is to be used, the regionality, aspects of the coverage, stimulus material and so on.

There is a tendency for these changes to be only informally recorded. This means that there may be no written final proposal, or to be more precise, no written specification of the work that has been agreed. This is surprisingly common but generally unsatisfactory as it can lead to confusion as to what the research was supposed to be. Obviously, where there is the possibility for confusion to exist it can do so either because of simple human error or by design. Although the research agency will be very clear what it is going to do, it is possible that with all the to-ing and fro-ing about that has gone on, the various client stakeholders may not be so clear what is finally going to happen, and this misunderstanding can have dramatic effects in the debrief! For this reason alone, it is always sensible to issue a final research specification as this removes any possibility of doubt – assuming of course that anybody reads it.

MANAGING THE PROJECT THROUGH FIELDWORK

Obviously, the fieldwork aspect of a research project is almost totally in the hands of the research supplier. However, the commissioner should abide by a few sensible rules.

Contactability

It is very important that the commissioner is easily contactable by the supplier. This is absolutely vital to the smooth progress of the project, as decisions may have to be made right across the duration of the project, which it is not possible for the agency to make by themselves. There are many ways this could happen: for example, the recruitment may be causing some problems and require adjustment in the light of this experience, the stimulus material may be wrong, weather conditions may affect the progress of the research and so forth.

Stimulus material

It is very important that materials required by the research agency get to them before the research take place. This is a fairly obvious statement, but is surprising how often this can cause a problem. In the case of quantitative research, the material may need to be repacked into a form suitable for the interviewers to use and then be distributed countrywide; this takes time and doing this late can add to cost.

In the case of qualitative research, it is not uncommon for the stimulus material to be sent directly to the first research location by courier. Not only does this mean the first group is often run without the benefit of the stimulus material because it had not arrived in time, but also that, even if it had, the researchers would have had little time to familiarize themselves with it before launching into the actual research. Neither situation helps to get quality qualitative research done.

In many cases it is sensible to have the stimulus material ready in order that it can be discussed at the research design stage with the researcher or agency. If the stimulus material is absolutely crucial to the research, such as a concept, pack or advert, it is generally very useful that the end-user client has actually seen it and formally agreed that it is what he or she expected. It is a dreadful waste of time and money as well as being very embarrassing if, as can occasionally happen, the wrong stimulus material is researched. Stimulus material is a constant source of problems, as described in Chapter 8.

Attendance at the research

Occasionally, the end-user client wishes to attend some aspect of the fieldwork. It is rare for a client to want to go out and about with a quantitative interviewer doing the interviewing, but if the research is held in a test hall the client might want to attend this, and clients are often quite keen to watch a group discussion in progress. Obviously end-user clients should be briefed as to what is expected of them, that they should be passive non-intrusive observers, leave the researchers to get on with their work, and not make 'helpful' comments to either the respondents or the interviewer.

These problems can be intensified in the case of people attending group discussions, because the very presence of observers can disturb the course of events. Viewers should be reminded that the respondents are people who have given up time to help them in their job and not objects of fun. The viewing should be taken seriously, and not thought of as a party. The sound of people laughing or making noises in the room behind an observation mirror does not put the respondents in a helpful frame of mind, is impolite, and is very disturbing to the researcher who is undertaking the difficult job of running the group.

Analysis needs peace and quiet

After the fieldwork has been completed, end-user clients are very keen to get the results, but as far as possible, they should restrain their impulses, as the very act of asking questions of the researcher can be counter-productive.

Ideally, by the end of the fieldwork, the researcher should have already given some indication of how the *process* actually went. This is the most basic feedback, and refers to things that are done and over with. However, when it comes to getting early feedback on the actual results, then the asking of this question is, in effect, asking the researcher to anticipate work yet to be done.

In the case of quantitative research, this question could lead to the data processing stage being run more quickly than was scheduled in order that 'top-lines' are available. If this has been planned in the original research design, then so be it. But if this question is just asked as a sudden afterthought, the work being requested will interfere with the flow of other work going through the agency and cause inefficiency, and even worse, mistakes.

It is at the early stage of quantitative analysis that 'funnies' can be resolved. These could be the result of some error in routing, a duff interviewer, data entry or data processing, and the process of accelerating the delivery time for 'top-lines' removes this safety check. In addition, 'funnies' can lead to very interesting 'top-line' conclusions if there is no time to think about them.

The situation is more pernicious in the case of qualitative research, as most end-user clients think that the findings are known before the last groups are completed. It is true, of course, that qualitatives researchers are formulating hypotheses about the research while they are actually in the progress of doing fieldwork, and may alter the lines of enquiry accordingly. However, this is a long way from 'knowing the answer'. This comes about as a result of a considerable amount of reflection and simply cannot be hurried.

The reason that asking qualitative researchers to give early feedback is very bad indeed, is that often they do not *know* what to say. Clearly they will have some impressions and some ideas, but the hard work of qualitative research is only just about to begin. This is the analysis stage, where an intellectual process is taking place with hypotheses emerging, being modified or put on one side until the researcher feels he or she has 'got it'. If he or she gives 'it' out before finishing this process, he or she may never 'get it', because the 'giving it out' itself fixes that part of the analysis. It is always best to leave researchers alone while they are doing analysis and to have programmed a sufficiently long period in the design for them to have two goes at it: that is, start the analysis, have a break, and then resume it. This is the way to get quality qualitative research done.

TRANSFERRING THE INFORMATION FROM THE RESEARCHER TO THE END-USER CLIENT

Preparing for the debrief

Some research managers want to actually go through the debrief before it is presented to the end-user client. This may be general practice for the particular company, or something that only happens occasionally: for example, when the presentation or the project (not necessarily the same thing) is high profile.

The researcher, on the other hand, might want to discuss the general findings with someone in the company before the debrief, in order to help formulate the final 'thing', or he or she might prefer to expose 'all' in the debrief without having given the finding out at all. Whatever the case, as has been mentioned before, it is important that end-user clients are pre-warned if there are likely to be controversial or unexpected find-ings, so that they can prepare themselves. It is also helpful to give the general 'feel' of the findings: for example, it seems good news.

Before the actual debrief takes place, the researcher should be informed who will be present and what their particular purpose for being there is, and what, if any, slant they may be bringing to the meeting. The actual debrief, no matter how low in profile, is always a performance in which, in many senses, the most important aspect of the whole process is taking place: that is, the transfer of the findings of the research to the client in a way that is understandable, believable and helpful. There is a lot of psychology in running the debrief.

THE ACTUAL DEBRIEF

Debriefs can take place in all sorts of environments, but it is preferable that there is a room that is quiet with plenty of space, sufficient chairs, and the means by which researchers can use whatever technology they want. This means that lighting, screens, places to put the stimulus material and any output from it (for example, respondent drawings), a projector that works and the other 'hygiene factors' are there. Often they are not, and it is disturbing to the psychology of what is going on if the researcher has to make do with inadequate facilities.

Researchers should be told in advance of any difficulties in access to the place of debrief (for example, difficulty in car parking), given clear directions and a contact number, and asked what help they need. Ideally they should be welcomed by the person who has commissioned the research, and given time to set up and make themselves comfortable.

The meeting will normally be chaired by the research commissioner (that is, the person who commissioned the research from the outside supplier), who can do the introductions and briefly position the research, remembering always that the attendees are there to hear the researcher, not the commissioner.

There can be problems with people coming in late, or tea or coffee arriving in the middle of the debrief. Both these things are very counter-productive and destroy the flow of the debrief. When it happens, it is generally best to stop the debrief until the disturbance is over. In the case of an attendee arriving late, a judgement has to be made about how much to delay the start of the debrief, and whether to recap if and when the person finally arrives. It is best to have already though this through before the commencement of the debrief.

Unfortunately, an attendee arriving late can be a deliberate policy to disrupt the debrief. As mentioned several times in this book already, the potency of market research can be most vividly displayed by the power politics that occasionally surround it.

Most researchers are happy to take questions as the debrief goes along, and in general it is the chair of the meeting's job to manage them. The issue here is that although questions can legitimately clarify something, they can also side-track the debrief, consuming time which puts pressure on the end, and worse, damage the coherency of the performance. Questions can also be constructed with a deliberate intent of destroying the integrity of the research findings. How questions are to be handled is best worked out between the researcher and the commissioner before the debrief starts.

The commissioner will often be looking at the attendees, trying to gather whether they are understanding what the researcher is saying in order that if they appear not to, he/she can strategically ask a question of the researcher to help clarify the point.

POST DEBRIEF

It is normal for the research to be reported in a form that can be used and understood by a person who had not attended the debrief. The historical way was for quite rigorous reporting to be done defining the sample, location, timings, something about the method, the 'narrative story' that had been discovered (if the research was qualitative) and the conclusions that flow from it. In the case of quantitative research, it was normal to support the findings with tables, and in the case of qualitative research to do the same using quotations from the transcripts.

It seems to be rare that this process is followed today. Instead, the research tends to be supported by 'debrief notes', which are often a printout of the presentation slides. Decisions can be, and often are, made in the debrief itself, but sometimes they are delayed as the information may be used as one part of the jigsaw puzzle, needing further reflection or to be put into a drawer until circumstances are right. The way that information is used after the debrief is the subject of Chapter 10.

CONCLUSION

The management of the research process takes many forms. At one end of the spectrum is the case of a regular supplier relating directly with the end-user who will manage the whole process him- or herself. At the other end will be a bureaucratic process run quite rigidly from the commissioning company. Both these models (and all stations in between) have their merits and demerits. In general, it is important to be clear about the objectives, have handled the politics surrounding the job, if any, and maintain good contact. Under these circumstances most jobs will be successful.

10 Managing the results

To many external researchers, the debrief is the end of the project, and in a number of instances this is also true for the commissioning company. This will be the case when a simple decision can be, and is, made in the debrief, or (for one of many reasons) a decision is made not to use the research at all. However, there can also be a lot of activity that follows the debrief when further work is done with it. This could be as simple as editing it before distribution, but it might be that the research's original purpose was to stimulate thinking in a creative way – and this naturally takes time and can lead to profound changes in direction for the project. Occasionally, though, there appears to be no action that follows the research and it appears to have failed. This is of particular interest (and concern), and the reasons that this sometimes happens are explored. Furthermore, there is the issue of trying to sustain the knowledge that has been gained through doing the research either by the use of some form of information system, more general circulation, or via the medium of the 'old retainer' – although, of course, this person may not actually be old. This chapter examines in detail the various options that follow the debrief.

KEY POINTS

- Most research projects are concluded at the debrief; this is because most projects are short-term tactical ones, and decisions are expected to be made, and are made, at the debrief time.

■ However, this is not always the case. Decisions may not be made because further work on the findings is required, or for some other less satisfactory reason.

■ These 'unsatisfactory reasons' could be because the purpose of the project has 'gone away', because the work was commissioned for political purposes to be used, if necessary, at some time in the future, or because it is seen to have failed.

■ More positive reasons for delaying a decision may be because the nature of the work was planned to be explorative and that there is now a need to think about the implications of the findings, the findings were surprising and need some reflection, or the findings need to be edited for the next stage of their use, for example, incorporation into a broader case that is to be made.

■ The archiving of the findings post-research is important but often done badly, especially now that the old research departments are being broken up. However, the new knowledge management systems that some companies are trying to introduce may help combat this waste.

■ The value of the quality archives come to the fore when the company conducts major strategic reviews. These are done when the company gets into a cul-de-sac, and is seeking ways out of it. At a more parochial level, archives are very valuable when the staff changes in an organization and the new people want to get up to speed in an area with which they may not be familiar.

HOW WAS IT FOR YOU?

The debrief has happened, the slides have been issued and the various client stakeholders in their different guises appear to be happy. Now what? There are three simple post-debrief scenarios:

■ The job delivers – the results have truly been action orientated and all the people who need to be involved were present and the decision was made.

■ The end-user has to do some further work with the data.

■ Nothing is done with the results at all and the research appears to have failed.

Each of these will now be considered in turn. The first is comparatively simple and will occupy little space, as this is the most common situation. The second outcome, which is also quite common, will be considered in detail. The third outcome will occupy even more space and concentrate particularly on the reasons that, on occasions, a project leads to no activity and appears to have failed.

The job delivers

The first scenario, that is, the job delivers, is common and really needs little comment, except that this scenario does not happen by accident. It happens because the right briefing led to a relevant design (see Chapter 8) that was well executed, analysed insightfully and the findings put across in a well-argued, convincing and relevant way. As has been stated again and again, it takes a lot of work to achieve this and, in truth, there also has to be a proper contribution from the client in terms of the briefing and in managing the politics (especially among the external stakeholders for the research findings, if any).

The end-user has to do some further work with the data

There are a number of reasons that there are cases when the debrief of a job is not the end but the beginning, and some more work has to be done. This could be because the work was *genuinely exploratory* and someone or some people now have to think about it, or that *it was always expected that only selective parts of it would be used* for incorporation with other data in order to complete a story.

These two main reasons for work being done after the debrief are explored in turn.

Exploratory work

It is not common for a piece of work to be commissioned purely for exploration. This implies that there is going to be some creative work done, but generally there is little time for this in an organization. Large organizations generally are in the continuous process of researching the market, and it is unlikely that any single project will cause a revolution to take place in the thinking. Consequently, this expectation will tend to be from a junior manager keen to make an impact and who therefore desperately wants to 'understand' the market or the brand in order to set his or her thinking going. More senior managers will rarely expect one piece or research to do this for them – they will have been through all this before and probably been disappointed. There are exceptions to this in terms of new product development, where little may be known about consumer feelings or expectations, and where genuinely new thinking is required. In these cases, the exploratory work will generally be taken up directly by a creative agency, which will have been a main stakeholder, and may even have already done some work on the project.

A 'story' for a specific purpose

Work may be done when a 'story' is being put together for a specific purpose. This could be to convince an internal body, such as a board, that a proposed course of action is sensible for constructing a sales launch, or organizing a sales pitch. Each of these cases will generally involve editing the data to simplify it and to make the case convincing.

There is a real problem in constructing these edited stories, especially if they involve more than one information source. The problem is that the most interesting conclusions are generally a matter of opinion. Market researchers, as a whole, are extremely concerned that they report the findings as they are, and work very hard to remove any aspect of their opinion. But when findings are edited, this is exactly what has to be done, as the editing process requires removing those aspects of the research that may imply a contradiction to the main findings. At its best, this is a responsible process that has the aim of adding clarity and brevity to the presentation, and it is actually a responsibility that market researchers are eminently qualified to undertake, but so often they do not. In part, the presence of this tendency in market researchers of all dispositions is the reason why the functions of 'advertising planning' and 'consumer insight' have grown up (see Chapter 4).

Clearly, in this editing process there is always the opportunity to pervert the course of justice, and to argue for something that is, in fact, not true. There is never a case when it is justified to create an edifice of lies, but in practice this is a moral question that is only ultimately resolved at the personal level – a person is happy to lie, or is not. In a sense this is a trite thing to say because in actuality there is a thin line to tread, and how closely one approaches this line depends upon the circumstances. The extremes are captured at one end by the case when a company has to make an objective decision as best that it can, and at the other where it is trying to sell an idea.

When a story is put together to help an internal decision, it should always be the case that the best attempt is made for the presentation to capture the absolute truth of the matter. Anything else is to pervert the very reason for doing market research in the first place. However, such stringent rules are not always applied when salespeople get their hands on the data. Clearly they are most concerned to put together a case to support their sales, whether it is the launch conference (to the sales force, for example) or a pitch to a retailer. In the case of a product launch to the sales conference, the salespeople, who are the target in this case, want to be convinced of the benefits of the new product and want to see conviction on the part of the marketing people who have put the whole thing together. It does no good to leave the sales force with any feelings of doubt. In the case of an account pitch, the receivers of the information are very familiar with the games that are played, and will generally equip themselves with the information to be able to ask difficult questions in order to get behind the 'spin'. It is very much the case of 'buyer beware', and everyone knows this.

The work may also be part of a programme of data collection that involves internal data analysis of sales or production information, market size and dynamics information, reviews of the brands in the market and of their advertising and so on, and the whole has to be combined into a single piece of work. This is complicated to do and generally involves a number of different research stakeholders. This appears to be a growth area and one in which companies are developing skills (Perrott, 1998). There is more about this type of activity in Chapter 11.

Nothing is done with the results of the research

There are a number of perfectly reasonable reasons for the results of a piece of research to lie fallow. First, and most common, is that the issue that originally required the research to be commissioned has gone away, and that there is now no reason to make use of it. The second reason is that the research had always been envisaged as a form of insurance policy to be pulled out of the drawer like some awful rabbit when necessary – so it was always going to be kept secret anyway. The third reason is that the research has failed in some way in the end-user's eyes, and therefore is unlikely to see the light of day. The last reason is especially interesting, and it will be dealt with in detail. However, first, let us look more closely at the first two reasons in more detail.

The job has gone away

There are many reasons that a job that was so urgent last week is now no longer necessary. There could be structural changes, such as the company being taken over, departments being reorganized, people being made redundant or leaving. There may be external activity involving a competitor, for example, launching the same product, or governmental activity in proposing to change the law. The world is in a continual state of flux and this occasionally influences research in the progress.

In cases where the need for the research has changed for rather small reasons, everyone tends to get a bit embarrassed and it can end up with people sitting around at the debrief making polite but uninterested noises, while trying to give the impression of involvement. In one respect, this is all the more difficult in the case of qualitative research as the person who has done all the work (pointlessly as it happens) is sitting in the same room, and as qualitative research involves such a lot of personal commitment on the part of the researcher, it seems a bit rude to suggest to him or her that the last two weeks of his or her life have been wasted.

Actually, this is all a bit misplaced as the researcher comes at it from quite a different perspective. In many cases, it is very difficult for researchers to know how the result of their work is ever used in the client company, and to them, the results often do not appear to be used anyway. In the case when the research is genuinely not now needed, the researcher will think of it as no more than a shame. Researchers have to develop an ability to cut off their involvement with their projects when they are finished, otherwise they would quickly go quite mad. The real difficulty, especially for qualitative researchers, is that when the research is 'pulled' after the fieldwork has been completed, the researcher tends not to know what is now expected of him or her. Should he or she trundle through a ridiculous charade of having to analyse and present the results (probably half-heartedly – researchers are human after all) and be told how interesting they are, or can he or she find a way of bringing it to a satisfactory conclusion that has at least some benefit to both parties? Researchers do not really like to have projects left in the air. In the case of quantitative research the situation is simpler: either the fieldwork is stopped, in which case there are no results, or the tables are sent in, perhaps with a simple (and probably trite) commentary.

The job is to be used for insurance

Some organizations are very political, and research is used as just one of many political instruments. 'Information is power', and there are some companies, in which the research is not properly organized or controlled, where it is very easy for research to be commissioned 'just in case'. For people who have worked supplying such companies, it is often apparent that the same research is commissioned on a number of different occasions, because different managers are marshalling separately their own weapons, or are working in ignorance or suspicion of one another.

The job is perceived to have failed

This is an interesting and complex area, and one where reputations are generally lost, but sometimes made. Broadly speaking there are three reasons for the job apparently not delivering:

- The research done was not what was expected would be done. There can be a number of reasons for this situation to occur.
- The findings are not believable to the end-user because the case for them has not been well made, probably because the chemistry between the researcher and the end-user was not of a nature to engender trust.
- The occasion (which is uncommon) when the research was actually not done well.

The next three sections examine these reasons in detail, starting with the most important one of all, that the job done was different from the one expected.

The research done was not what was expected

The most obvious reason for the job being different from what was expected is that the briefing stage failed. Much has already been written about the need to get the briefing correct (see Chapter 8), and researchers are very sensitive to not getting misbriefed. Danger points are when the briefing has been remote, the situation has changed and no one has told the research commissioner, or the end-user has changed midstream. Research managers have to be always on their guard to ensure that these things do not happen, that they do not take at face value what they are being told in all cases, and they ensure that the documentation is properly written – not that this will be of much help when the disaster happens.

It is worth expanding on the situation when the end-user has changed midstream, and a new one has come in after some research has been commissioned. The new end-user can often not appreciate what was briefed into the research, and is expecting something quite different. This situation is easy to get into. Marketing people change all the time, and new ones are taking in a lot of information during their induction, so it is easy for them to think that the research is about something different from what it actually is. When this happens the marketing manager will become really disappointed, as he or she may have built the research up as being something capable of resolving all the immediate misunderstandings and confusions. The research commissioner should be aware that this could happen and try to get the new person involved with it so that he/she can fully understand what is going on. It is not good to start a relationship with a failure even though it is a result of a legitimate misunderstanding on the client side.

Occasionally, there is a genuine misalignment between what the client expects and the researcher delivers. When it happens (which is not often), the fact that the researcher has done what he or she said would be done in the proposal tends not to carry much weight. The end-users are, of course, far too busy to bother with actually reading the proposal let alone think about it. The fact is, as the end-users see it, the results are not forthcoming, and one way or another this is generally seen to be the fault of the researcher. Protesting does not do too much good either, because if the client is in fact to blame, he or she most certainly does not want to be told so. However, these are the occasions when internal researchers show their mettle by siding with the researcher and supporting him or her in time of need (or not, as the case may be), and trying to make the best of what has been done.

The research findings are not believed

The second reason that the results from the research may not be acted on is that the end-user client simply *does not believe that they are correct*. This may occur for one of two reasons: when the case for the findings has not been made convincingly, or the findings are way out of line with expectations.

As has been stated a number of times in this book (see especially Chapter 8), it is very important that end-users feel they can relate to researchers in believing in their skills, and (especially if the research is qualitative), that the personal chemistry is right. This is very unfair and verges on the unprofessional, but is very much part of the common idea encapsulated in the phrase 'Would you buy a second-hand car from this person?'. Given the care that should have been put into ensuring that there was a good match between the end-user client and the researcher or research agency, this problem only tends to arise when the end-user client has changed during the course of the research.

The end-user may feel very uncomfortable for other comparatively trivial reasons, for example, if there are too many silly mistakes in the research. Typically these are spelling mistakes, simple arithmetical mistakes or misuse of terminology with the view being taken that if these things which the end-user client can check are wrong, what value can be put on the findings that cannot be checked? The presence of these mistakes also plays directly into the hands of people who may want to rubbish the research for political reasons (see Chapter 9). One of the reasons that some research managers prefer to go through the research with the researcher is precisely to eradicate these small things that can easily blow up into a big issue and be used to invalidate the findings of the research.

The other common reason that the end-user client may not accept the results is that they seem to be so far from what is perceived to have been the case historically, even though the case for them has been well made. In truth, this is a good reason to be suspicious of the results, especially if the company engages in continual market research, but when the research is the first that has been done, then it may actually be truly revolutionary and iconoclastic. The problem here is that the end-user client will generally be new to research and inexperienced in handling it, and even worse, will have a lot of personal identity wrapped up in his or her particular insight into the market. It is very difficult for such an end-user client to have an identity crisis in the middle of a debrief, and he or she will normally choose not to – by saying all the findings are wrong! Obviously, this situation can be managed by letting the end-user know something of the results before the debrief, and also by briefing the researcher as to the expectations.

The research was of poor quality

The final reason the job does not deliver is that the work actually was not done well. This is rare, as it is not possible to be a successful researcher by chance – to sustain themselves in employment, researchers and the organizations behind them have to be competent. In practice, researchers are dedicated people who really do care about the work they are doing, and really want to deliver quality results. So when the work is done badly it is generally a result of some external factor coming into play.

Work may be done badly because the researcher has taken on too much, often as a favour to help someone out, or when the client has changed the timing of the job so that it now clashes with a previously planned one to the detriment of both, or because the job has proved more taxing in fieldwork because of, for example, unexpected bad weather, clients not setting up those things they were supposed to, or because the issues proved more complex at the analysis stage and thinking time ran out, and so on.

But sometimes they just fail; researchers are human after all. They are just as likely as the rest of us to get ill or have personal problems and yet battle on. Occasionally a researcher just gets fed up with doing research and needs to do something else but has not yet made the change. This is rare, and is more likely to happen in the case of qualitative research than quantitative. When failure occurs, it is likely to be that a combination of things happened at once. Market research has its fair share of having to handle the unexpected and juggle a variety of issues simultaneously, but there can be a limit!

So it can be seen that there are many reasons for a job to be perceived to have failed, and that the majority of them are outside the control of the researcher. However, the internal researcher should, and often does, work to anticipate these possible scenarios, and intervene to prevent them materializing.

INCORPORATION OF THE RESEARCH INTO THE KNOWLEDGE OF THE BUSINESS

This final section looks at the ways companies try to preserve the information that they are collecting. The huge advantage that accrues from being able actually to build knowledge in the company was discussed in Chapter 2, where knowledge was positioned as the ultimate source of value of a company. Knowledge management is a real growth industry, as various suppliers and users grapple with the difficulty of building, managing and sustaining a company's knowledge. In practice, companies do not currently do this at all well, and the methods used are mostly of the obvious and traditional type. These are elaborated in the following subsections, but we start with the most pedestrian method of them all – reports.

Reports

Knowledge can only be preserved if it is documented in a coherent way, and in terms of research this used to mean writing a report. The format of a report is modelled on that of the scientific paper, and this requires that researchers adequately report the research in a form that makes sense when it is read a year (or 10 years) later. This can be achieved if the document satisfies the basics for reporting as described in the Code of Conduct of the MRS. This covers such things as the timing, research design (including the sample), a description of the stimulus material used (difficult if it is a reel of adverts, or a set of packs), and explaining such matters as why the research was done, as well as the meat of the research – the findings themselves.

The standards of reporting have changed in recent years (some might say fallen) in response to a lack of interest on the part of the client (that is, not demanding it) which, coupled with the time and diligence it takes on the part of the researcher to complete, has meant that in many cases the only report available is the printed-out version of the slides, which at best can only act as a memory prompt to people who had attended the debrief. One of the reasons for this is the boring nature of reports written in the way they are 'supposed' to be and the lack of adventure in proposing conclusions. However, once this has been said, it is sensible if the debrief notes attempt to contain the obvious information about the actual research that was done as well as the findings of it.

In many cases there seems, at the time of the debrief, to be no reason why a report should be written. The job was simple, fast and achieved its objectives, and a decision was made. So why have a report? The answer to this is that there is probably additional information that has been collected and interpreted on the way to the main findings, and this is of value to people in the company in understanding the market and the brands better. Furthermore, the decisions taken following the debrief may be questioned at some point, and it is of value to have some form of supporting documentation.

Archiving

Given the considerable sums of money that are spent on market research by large companies, it would seem pretty obvious that getting it reported and archived would be no more than a prudent way of enhancing the value to be obtained from this expenditure. Often, archived reports are not accessed for some time after the project. However, they come into their own when there is a change of personnel: new people always want to read the old research. If the reports have been well written with appropriate background, the set of them should provide a unique insight into the thinking about the market and the marketing that has taken place. This can be as helpful to the new person as the actual information contained in the reports about the brands and the market. Another value of archiving research is when major market reviews are conducted, frequently at a time when the market is 'on the turn' or major changes are in the offing. Properly reported research can really help the company not make the same mistakes again, and can provide a real competitive advantage over those companies that have not been through this discipline.

The idea of archiving implies that there are some archives somewhere. This is a big assumption, as without an active function to achieve this, even those archives that exist will not have anything in them – the items will have been borrowed, never to be seen again. Even operating a library is a real nightmare. Someone has to know that some research has taken place, and then they have to extract the report (if one exists) from the commissioner, then document it and file it. Libraries are (inevitably) political – who has access to what for example. The proper way to run an archive is to have a librarian to do this specialized job, but few companies do. More often there is a filing cabinet full of the stuff in varying states of disarray. In companies that have a centralized market research department, it is much more likely that a library that works is maintained. However, as companies reorganize, get taken over, takeover other companies or merge, the archives are likely to be misplaced or destroyed. So what appears to be very simple is, in practice, very hard to maintain. All of this is very sad, as the ability to move on depends upon having some preservation of current and historic knowledge.

In principle, many of these problems can be overcome by using simple company intranet methods. These certainly get over problems of reports being lost (until the IT department wants the storage space reduced!), but they do not resolve the political issues (which may actually grow through the greater ease of getting the information) or the problem of properly resourcing a function to do it.

Making the knowledge more widely available

Some companies try to summarize research as it is done and circulate this among relevant parties, so that there is wide awareness of what has been done. Obviously this stops the same research being commissioned twice (or even three times), but in reality, most research is so task oriented, it is mostly only of interest to the commissioner, and therefore the 'interesting' material inevitably gets summarized out! There is also a problem in that people are inundated with information, and summaries of research that bear no relevance to one's job are generally not welcome.

A more contemporary method is to use the passive approach of placing the information on the company intranet. Knowledge management systems are much better able to handle this information, provided the information is put in. In principle it is possible to search for relevant documents using a search engine, and get summaries or the whole documents online. As already stated, few companies have implemented systems at this level of sophistication yet, although there is a great deal of activity in this area. Chapter 2 describes the different approaches to knowledge management.

Information management – the old retainer

By far the easiest-to-use method of knowledge management is to have the 'old retainer' who has lived through a thousand and one debriefs, and can remember what has been done. Furthermore, the 'old retainer' is able to synthesize a knowledge base in a way that is quite unique, culling gems of information from one pedestrian piece of work after another. Of course the 'old retainer' does not actually have to be old, only to have been around for long enough, and the author personally knows of an 'old retainer' who is under 30 years of age.

CONCLUSION

Although many research debriefs are effectively the end of the matter, in that a decision (mostly of the tactical type) is taken actually in the debrief, some work generally follows it within the company. In the ordinary course of things, the amount of work done subsequently is not extensive – being some sort of editing, communication of the findings and archiving.

11 Knowing the future

Occasionally, companies want to look to the future to redefine their strategy. They could be envisaging some form of major restructuring of the company, involving selling bits of it off or buying other companies, in which case they are very likely to turn to a management consultancy for help. Alternatively, they may be looking to find opportunities in their own or related markets, or they may be looking to revitalize a brand. Under these circumstances they will choose a consumer-led method that will by necessity involve market research. This will require bringing together different data sources and coming to some consensus as to their meaning.

KEY POINTS

■ Organizations are sometimes confronted with the need to examine the future so that they can develop an appropriate strategy to address it. To enable them to do this they will need to adopt some form of process.

■ The process may be run from outside the organization or be an internal project. One important advantage of using an outside organization is that a labour force is available to make the project happen. However, the difficulty with using an outside organization is in getting emotional commitment to the findings of the project when internal people have not been a part of it.

- The process the company adopts will be coloured by its expectations of the outcome. Management consultancies tend to be used when it is expected that the structure of the company will change, and the 'solution' will have a heavy financial component to it. Consumer-led approaches are use when market or brand opportunities are sought, and it is in this case that considerable market research is involved.
- Processes used to examine the future can be positioned on a 'safe to risky' spectrum, and the one that is selected will depend upon the company culture. There is safety with using external people with a reputation for engaging in the future and by using numerically supported trend data. Risk is associated with using creative methods, inventing conceptual factors that drive the market and applying them to it in an imaginative way.
- The principle of 'making one's own future' is rarely considered, as this involves leadership and courage.

INTRODUCTION

In Chapter 3 it was stated that organizations could generally handle catastrophic change better than adapting to the slow transformation of the world. They can fail to notice the significance of the changes in the short term and end up in a mess in the long term. When this happens, the company starts to feel that it has reached a cul-de-sac, a sense of unease and frustration sets in, and it cannot think which way it should be going. This can occur at an organizational level (how can it position itself better to achieve growth – should the organization be selling bits of itself off, buying other companies, or what?), at a market level (what are the opportunities in this market or related ones, and how should they be addressed?) or at a brand level (how can this brand be revitalized or extended?).

The sense of impotence that a company can feel can radically influence what the company does as it loses confidence in itself. For example, the control of the marketing may start to move, by default, to the advertising agencies, with the expectation that *stunning* new advertising will be the 'solution'. Alternatively, the budget for marketing is cut, resources move over to operations and the company starts thinking of itself as a financial instrument. This means that it stops looking at the consumer altogether and moves to selling a commodity or at the very best an 'est' brand (see Chapter 1). This tends to be the consequence of doing nothing, and is also the likely outcome when one employs a management consultancy. This route does have the advantage of preserving the bottom line, which is the only concern the company's owners have if it is primarily financed by equity. It is, of course, absolutely essential that the company makes money, as that is primarily what it is for (see Chapter 1), but it is still a depressing outcome when it is achieved in this way.

An alternative to this scenario is to try to find a consumer-led way out of the box, but the problem is how to do this. All the obvious areas of exploration have been done, there *is* a great deal of knowledge in the company, but fundamental questions about the market may be being raised which are virtually impossible to answer by going directly to the consumers and asking them.

Market research is, of course, actually about the *past* and is particularly applicable to helping with decisions that relate to the *now*. This is why much market research is unashamedly short term and tactical. Even research that is aimed at strategic development is really about the now, and draws conclusions from a very detailed examination of the status quo. So the question is how all the information about people, customers and consumers that has been built up over the years can be utilized to help an organization formulate a consumer led strategy.

THINKING ABOUT A CONSUMER-LED FUTURE

The nature of the work done depends very much on the culture of the organization. It can be handed to an outside organization or be done internally, and it can be done in a fairly conservative way or imaginative methods can be used. Each of these approaches has its merits and demerits, and actually is applicable in different situations.

The work can be commissioned outside with a futures organization, which may be one that specializes in this sort of activity, or more commonly a management consultancy. This is a safe decision to make as the external organization (of either type) will have a reputation and track record, and this therefore appeals to cultures that are risk-adverse. Management consultants will also include a financial dimension in what they do and finally report, and this can be appealing to a board that thinks it might be heading for trouble. Another advantage of using an external organization is that a labour force is available for deployment in driving the project forward. Typically, the process involves quite extensive interviewing with internal staff, followed by some sort of experiential stage where the people concerned immerse themselves in an aspect of the market, followed by a data assembly stage and an analysis of all the information, from which a strategy is formed. The disadvantage to the organization is that the organization does actually have to spend *a lot of time* on this, especially those people in the information areas, so the labour force issue becomes a problem. Furthermore, there is the problem of getting the overall strategy emotionally accepted by the company, and external organizations tend to use their reputation (and the fact that the invoice is very high) as a lever to do this.

If the process is to be conducted internally, then it will need very heavyweight support to actually galvanize people into action – this is not something to take on lightly. A team will need to be assembled that includes the various stakeholders. This should comprise people from the marketing team and their associated agencies as well as people from various relevant functions such as R&D and operations. The problem is limiting the team to a reasonable size, not only because the bigger the team, the more difficult it is to get them all together at one time, but also because creative methods tend to work better when used with smaller groups. The advantage of doing this all internally is that the stage of getting up to speed (which is necessary when using an outside organization) is short-circuited, saving time, money and effort. However, a difficulty of doing this internally is the ability to drive the work to a satisfactory conclusion – there are too many other things to do.

The particular approach that the company adopts (either using outside people or running the process internally) can lie anywhere along the pedestrian-creative axis, and will mirror the culture of the organization. Some organizations are very risk-adverse and a bit stodgy, and organizations such as these will always want to work in a way that is manifestly logical. Others may be quite happy to be very speculative and, for example, use group projective exercises to help achieve their end.

This author has a preference of undertaking these processes internally and being as creative as possible. The reason for this preference is that it is easier to get access internally to people who have a really genuine contribution to make, and who will become committed to the outcome as the journey proceeds. From a creative point of view, there is also the matter that if the company does not know what to do, then it will not find the answer using logical methods, as these will already have been applied.

A process for looking at the future

There are four main stages in doing this difficult and important exercise. The first stage is to get some idea of the factors that are operating in the market and how they may change in the immediate and distant future. The second stage is to extract the meaning of these changes to the market, the third stage is to formulate a strategic approach to these anticipated changes, and finally there is a need to persuade the organization to buy in to this strategy. Implementation of the strategy is then done through the normal agencies used by the company. Actually, the fourth stage of getting buy-in is not really a fourth stage at all, as it cannot be bolted on at the end, and tends to be a feature that is considered all the way through the process. Each of these stages is considered below.

Factors affecting the market: formulating the 'trends'

It is important to take into account the social and economic trends that are likely to impact the markets in the future – whether they generate more of the same needs or spawn completely different ones. Developing such a view is clearly vital to understanding the value of future markets and thinking about how best to address them.

A fairly safe way of doing this is to list some trends (often well-documented economic, demographic and social trends), that seem important, extrapolate them into the future by drawing a straight line graph and ask questions as to their significance (if any). As a method of short-range forecasting this is reasonably sound, and was the process advocated by Henley in the 1980s. The reason that this process is safe is that it unashamedly quantitative and therefore is underpinned by the numbers so liked by contemporary organizations (see Chapter 6).

The basic problem with this approach is that it assumes three things that, at best, can only be partially true: trends are linear and therefore immutable, the only trends usable and therefore worth worrying about are those that are documented, and the future is *ordained* and not *made*.

An alternative to this process, or preferably an addition to it, is the use of *conceptual* trends. These can be arrived at by buying into a proprietary futures system, which is generally quantitative and has some history about the way trends are moving. Furthermore, since it is established and known, the futures system is likely to have some credibility within an organization. Alternatively, one can arrive at conceptual trends through qualitative research, especially semiotic research, which seeks out trends as a primary part of the method (Alexander, 2000).

However, a more interesting way to do this is to invent the trends oneself by considering the knowledge that lies in the organization and arriving at a view about changes (that seem particularly relevant to one's market) that are happening in the world. It is easier, and certainly much better, to do this with a group of people chosen from what would be the equivalent of the research stakeholders if the process had been researched. Not only does this bring to bear an important and committed knowledge base, it also helps with the ultimate buy-in to the outcome of the process.

Normally an early stage to this is to share experiences and information. This is an important stage, but at the same time it should not have too much emphasis placed on it. The range of inputs might be extracts from a number of research studies or other data sources, or might be reports on softer, more stimulating experiences, such as the examination of alternative markets, or perhaps visiting another country (typically, the United States). The participants could also be asked to do something that they would not normally do, for example, actually buy some of the products they are responsible for and see what the experience of both buying and using the product is like, or perhaps even live for a short time with the consumers they expect to influence. These experiences can then be reported back to the group, and the process is generally facilitated by an external person to ensure that it runs in a satisfactory way. The purpose of all this activity is to get people into a common frame of mind in which the brain has been loosened up.

One important part of this process is working with formal quantitative information. As was mentioned at the beginning of this chapter, most market research, and for that matter market analysis, is carried out for short-term tactical reasons, and therefore the bulk of the company's information will be in that form, unless the company has attempted to build an 'information climate' (see Chapter 2). Either way, there will need to be some form of extrapolation of the data, and this can only be achieved by using creative methods. This type of work seems to be getting more common, and the skills for doing it are being developed at the moment (Shields, 2001).

Typically, facilitation of the group will draw on creative meeting methods, and qualitative researchers have a whole gamut of techniques that are helpful in this, although meeting facilitators generally have developed bespoke skills for this purpose. The sort of techniques used range from simple structured brainstorming (for example brainstorming against a series of questions), to methods aimed at getting to the 'primary dimensions' such as grouping sticky notes with ideas on, using 'laddering' methods (why is this important?), or 'break-out' methods using classic projective techniques such as drawing and storytelling.

Trends developed in this way, being conceptual and specifically devised for the purpose in hand, are in principle very potent in helping to construct a relevant future because they allow more creative solutions to be adopted. However, such trends do not have the formal validity that well-documented ones do, and are therefore easily challenged by people within the company who may wish to question the process. People can become very unsettled when major changes in the direction of the company are in the air, and power politics are very likely to emerge (see Chapter 3).

As an illustration, some examples of such conceptual trends (used by the author in the past) are listed below:

- **Peace and prosperity.** It seems that the western world has reached an unusual position that could well provoke change on a grand scale. There has never before been such a long period of peace, in which sustained economic growth has taken place and allowed major social changes to occur.
- **Material wealth.** Furthermore, there are important structural changes happening to consumerism that seem to be driven by the level of sheer wealth that is now increasingly common. There really is a limit to the extent to which people can surround themselves with material goods, and in this context the fear of making poor purchasing decisions is lower, as the consequences of doing so become of little material importance. Interestingly, this should

mean that there is a trend to buying 'better' (whatever that will mean), rather than 'more'.

- **Two people working per family.** The stresses of the modern world and the trend of two people working to support a family have meant a considerable growth in products aimed at removing as many chores as possible, but again there is a limit to all of this. Buying things can itself be a chore because it involves engaging the brain.
- **Anti-capitalism.** The emergence of the European Union with its tradition of social democracy will inevitably act as a counterbalance to the dominant capitalist tradition of the last few centuries in a way that communism failed to do. Wealth and stability may well lead to the traditional work ethic being questioned, and greater value attributed to other aspects of human endeavour. For example, the substantial reduction in birth rate over the last few decades (which is likely to undermine the economic success of Europe into the future) looks like a manifestation of materialism, and it is possible that this may start to be reversed if society re-evaluates its basic tenets.

The reason that these trends have been included here is not that they have particular general validity, but they are an illustration of opening up thinking about the future.

Extracting meaning from the trends

Once the process of identifying a series of relevant trends is complete, it is important to identify the 'therefore' that they imply in the market. If these trends have been identified internally, the emergence of the 'therefores' will have been happening simultaneously with the identification of the trends. Indeed this process can generate an enormous amount of enthusiasm, and a type of religious belief in the work develops. This is valuable (in that it achieves the difficult objective of buy-in) but dangerous (as the thoughts may be too uncritical), and it is sensible to undertake a process of *scenario development* in which alternative possible futures are developed. This means that the trends are put together differently, and ideally one should seek to develop a future that is optimistic about the market, one that is pessimistic and another that is neutral. The great advantage of building scenarios at this stage is that it allows trends that have been developed separately to be put together and be seen as a coherent group. This also allows for the sense of them as a set to be experienced and, by implication, challenged.

However, the point of scenario development is that the impossible becomes debatable. For example, material wealth might not continue to grow because most people have enough and are now prepared to trade off the prospect of more wealth (with its perceived diminishing returns) against another things – spirituality, for example. Another accepted 'fact' might be that neighbourhood shopping centres have shown continued decline, and that therefore such shopping environments do not have any retail future. But why have they experienced a decline? Could it be because an increasing amount of women have been going out to work over the last 20 years, and that therefore there have been less shoppers available to use the neighbourhood shopping centre? How will teleworking impact on this? Will more people work in their own home environment in the future? Will local communities start growing and developing in a social sense, and what does this mean to retailing?

Actually, the number of companies that go to the trouble of developing full-scale scenarios appears to be very small, but there are lessons that can be taken from the process and used for more modest 'adventures' into the future.

Building consensus using workshops

The whole process of thinking about the future in order to help in the development of the company's strategy, or the next stage of evolution of its products, means that it is necessary to work with groups of people in the company, primarily to use their individual knowledge, but also to build a consensus. Consensus is a powerful way of getting different parties aligned to a particular course of action, and in the process of achieving this real use is made of the knowledge that already exists in the company.

One of the problems with working to build a set of trends and to interpret their potential impact on the market (as described in the previous section) is that only certain companies have a culture capable of making this happen. As mentioned earlier in this chapter, an early stage of the project involves working with data in an attempt to use it to build a broader picture. Many business people feel comfortable with playing with the data, but people vary in the degree to which they are prepared to extrapolate from it. It is important that the degree to which this is done fits the culture of the organization, as it is not sensible to try to put people in a position where they do not feel comfortable. Indeed, this would be totally counter-productive.

The individual methods described above are not particularly important; of much more importance is that there is a clear plan as to how the series of meetings are run and what each part is expected to achieve. Gaining consensus about the desired outcomes is generally the critical stage.

TAKING CONTROL AND DETERMINING THE FUTURE

This chapter has been about trying to understand what the future is likely to be like, and is playing on an assumption that the future is in some way *ordained*, while it is common experience that it is *made* – humankind does a lot to determine its own future. Indeed the success of science is that it enables humankind to do just this. Similarly, it should be possible for a company to determine its own future to some extent, and certainly it can determine the future as it affects its own brands. This requires the application of leadership and determination rather than worrying too much about what is going on. In a sense, what is important here is to ensure that the company's strategy is not going *against* the inevitable, rather than to worry about being swept along with inevitable changes.

Examples of the future being changed by the arrival of a new product are not uncommon, and every now and then a new product arrives and changes the scene forever. Furthermore, the new product often has an impact that was not expected, and society restructures around the changes that flow from it. An example of this was the arrival of large freezer units for consumers, which were sold on the basis that it would be possible to buy in bulk and save money. In practice this hardly ever happened, and freezers are used today to manage time: that is, the time of shopping can be disconnected from the time of cooking. Microwaves are another well-known example, as is the story of the Walkman; the significance of the current telecom revolution hardly needs discussing.

This leads one to question the value of doing either classic or conceptual trend analysis at all, but suggests that rather the problem should be approached from the other way round: that is, to generate speculative ideas and explore their vitality in terms of the trends, to see which might actually have the greatest chance of impacting on the nature of the future. However, only the most visionary companies could contemplate this, and in general these do not exist amongs current large corporations.

CONCLUSION

Companies sometimes need to start considering the future. This can be because they have not been properly in contact with the world outside the company, which has been changing slowly and unnoticed around them, so that they are now in danger of becoming stranded. Alternatively, companies may be considering the future precisely to avoid becoming out of date and to maintain a contemporary position.

The way in which they approach this problem depends very much on the nature of the perceived solution and also the culture of the company itself. They may turn to outside agencies or they may do it themselves, and the nature of the project could be highly financial in orientation or consumer led. It could also be very risk free in its approach, or speculative and creative.

Depending on how these factors come together in a particular case, market research and the information that comes from it can have varying degrees of input. Managing the collection of the information from a variety of sources to produce a coherent view and an input to all this is not easy.

12 Conclusion

This book has been about the practicalities of handling market research from within a company, and has focused on this being undertaken by large commercial organizations in which there is a defined function to manage it. As the reader will now be aware, the material in this book has probably never been written down before, although there is wide acceptance of the truth of it. One advantage of articulating these matters is that it makes it easier for them to be more openly discussed; for too long now market research has been held to be a logical process, whereas it is rife with all the failings that affect other human endeavours.

A list of principles follows for producing a successful market research function within an organization:

- Organizations have to make decisions in order to stay alive, and these decisions often involve understanding their customers. Market research is an important way in which this can be achieved provided that the output of its various components are managed as a coherent whole. When this is done, market research and the function that manages it can develop an information climate that facilitates decisions and helps innovation. Therefore, market research is a critical function in a company, especially if it is producing value added brands rather than commodities or 'est' brands. The most important action that the market research function performs is to establish and maintain this belief. This requires constant attention as to how the research group is perceived as well as constant selling of 'the message'.

- Maintenance of a successful market research group requires that the group stays out of the politics, while being very sensitive to them. It is very important indeed to sustain an image of integrity, and the easiest way by far of doing this is genuinely to have integrity.
- Within the organization there are many people who are in a state of stress. This is generally because the levels of work required these days are very high. The disadvantage of this is that it reduces the efficiency of an organization and people make mistakes. Furthermore, people often have no time to think things through, so one cannot be expected to take what people say at face value. Life would be much easier if this were not the case, but unfortunately it is. The market research function can win a lot of friends by recognizing this and trying to help those people in distress. This means actually trying to accommodate this stress, and not being difficult when briefs come in late, e-mails are not responded to or people change their minds again and again.
- When power politics raises their ugly head, it is rare that they do so blatantly, so it is very important to be constantly on the lookout for them. People can become very disagreeable when decisions go against them, and are likely to attack the researcher or the research function. This is all in a day's work, but can be fatal if not handled well. The greatest defence to this is to anticipate these attacks and work to neutralize them before they become manifest. This is generally possible because people on the whole will not admit to being motivated by anything other than the rational good of the company.
- It is of great importance to have a group of suppliers that suit the organization, and these can only be built up over a long period of time. It goes without saying that suppliers should be properly and considerately treated. This means having some knowledge of the difficulties that they face and trying not to make these difficulties any worse than they otherwise would be. High on the list is giving suppliers the time required to do the job, the information that they need to do it, and just as important, the information when they need it, not a day (or so) later. In order to understand the market of research products and people in the profession, it is very important to keep in contact with the industry. This means allowing people to pitch, attending conferences, reading papers and connecting with the gossip. All this is vital in order to perform the role of a research buyer.

- It is proper that a large buyer in the market should try to help move the market on. This means having a budget to do so, and this is not easy to achieve. However, if the company really does believe in the research function, this budget is a tangible manifestation of that belief. Ideally the company will want to do research at the leading edge of the market and to have the advantages this brings over the competition.

- Staff development is important from many standpoints. Not only does it contribute to the ability of people in the industry (as staff will always move on), it is also an exciting way of developing new products. A major buyer should also try to be engaged with its suppliers' staff in terms of personnel secondments or just by going to talk to them. This is obviously a two-way process as how else will a buyer, who may never have worked in a research agency, know what goes on deep inside it?

All the above principles contribute to being part of a successful research function. The following are a few thoughts about changes that may take place in the future.

- Market research does not stand still, and one has to keep an eye on what is just round the corner. This book is unusual in stating the view that there is absolutely no difference between the quality of information of a qualitative nature and that of a quantitative nature, although they are clearly different in kind and fit for different purposes. As described, qualitative research has gained ground, rather grudgingly, because it delivers what quantitative research cannot, but the schizophrenic view about it continues.

- There are moves to be more holistic in the interpretation of quantitative research (which suffers from a question-by-question analysis framework) and to take a more cavalier attitude to the caveats that have traditionally been applied to its findings. This looks rather like taking on qualitative clothes, and to a certain extent is obviously to the good, but there is a danger in this. Doing quality quantitative research is very hard (as also is doing quality qualitative research). With a growing view that all the caveats are tedious rubbish comes the possibility that not only will they not be mentioned, but also they will not be applied to the research, so there could be a problem about knowing whether the work that will be done in the future is going to be of a proper quality. Furthermore, as quantitative research is not that easy to understand properly there could be a tendency to actually throw out the use of quantitative research in its entirety as all being too boring to cope with (as some advertising agency planners currently appear to be doing). Clearly this would be unfortunate.

- There could be a revival of quantitative research – what I have called the 'new quantitative research'. This is the because of the increasing amount of information available from company systems that could be leveraged by combining it with external quantitative data. There are signs of this happening already where external data is attached to customers' data from a loyalty card scheme: for example, of data attached to a customer's phone or other utility records.

- One of the greatest opportunities with new quantitative research is the ability to model it mathematically. The modelling of quantitative data is on the increase mainly because of the greater availability of computers than there was just 10 years ago. Modelling allows a more holistic approach to be taken (because a number of individual characteristics will be used in the model), it allows a greater simplification of the data (often to a simple spreadsheet) and it allows 'what if' questions to be asked. In principle there is no reason why these models should not be operating in real time and become an integral part of the process control of the company.

- This possible future will depend on organizations getting to grips with their entire information in an integrated way. As mentioned earlier, vast amounts of information are being collected at the moment by companies and being stored either on departmental spreadsheets or within company databases. At the moment the manner in which analysis is conducted on departmentally held data has to be questioned, as there is no reason this should be done well. As for the case of system-held data, at the moment this is largely impossible to access, although the situation is slowly changing. The move to the creation of customer insight departments could herald the recognition that there is more information in the company than financial and sales analysis or market research, but this whole area is up for grabs.

This chapter has reviewed the basic contents and messages of this book. Probably the book has concentrated too much on what is difficult and what is not right. Actually there is a lot that is right in the industry and in the way it works, and there is a tremendous amount of fun and fulfilment to be had. Fortunately, it looks as if there are fantastic opportunities ahead. They will not be easy to seize and make happen, but then nothing that is worthwhile is.

Appendix: The Market Research Society Code of Conduct

INTRODUCTION

The Market Research Society

With over 8,000 members in more than 50 countries, The Market Research Society (MRS) is the world's largest international membership organisation for professional researchers and others engaged in (or interested in) marketing, social or opinion research.

It has a diverse membership of individual researchers within agencies, independent consultancies, client-side organisations, and the academic community, and from all levels of seniority and job functions.

All members agree to comply with the MRS Code of Conduct, which is supported by the Codeline advisory service and a range of specialist guidelines on best practice.

MRS offers various qualifications and membership grades, as well as training and professional development resources to support these. It is the official awarding body in the UK for vocational qualifications in market research.

MRS is a major supplier of publications and information services, conferences and seminars and many other meeting and networking opportunities for researchers.

MRS is 'the voice of the profession' in its media relations and public affairs activities on behalf of professional research practitioners, and aims to achieve the most favourable climate of opinions and legislative environment for research.

The purpose of the 'Code of Conduct'

This edition of the Code of Conduct was agreed by The Market Research Society to be operative from July 1999. It is a fully revised version of a self-regulatory code which has been in existence since 1954. This Code is based upon and fully compatible with the ICC/ESOMAR International Code of Marketing and Social Research Practice. The Code of Conduct is designed to support all those engaged in marketing or social research in maintaining professional standards. It applies to all members of The Market Research Society, whether they are engaged in consumer, business to business, social, opinion or any other type of confidential survey research. It applies to all quantitative and qualitative methods for data gathering. Assurance that research is conducted in an ethical manner is needed to create confidence in, and to encourage co-operation among, the business community, the general public, regulators and others.

The Code of Conduct does not take precedence over national law. Members responsible for international research shall take its provisions as a minimum requirement and fulfil any other responsibilities set down in law or by nationally agreed standards.

The purpose of guidelines

MRS Guidelines exist or are being developed in many of these areas in order to provide a more comprehensive framework of interpretation. These guidelines have been written in recognition of the increasingly diverse activities of the Society's members, some of which are not covered in detail by the Code of Conduct. A full list of guidelines appears on the Society's website, and is also available from the Society's Standards Manager.

One particular guideline covers the use of databases containing personal details of respondents or potential respondents, both for purposes associated with confidential survey research and in cases where respondent details are passed to a third party for marketing or other purposes. This guideline has been formally accepted by the Society, following extensive consultation with members and with the Data Protection Registrar/Commissioner.

Relationship with data protection legislation

Adherence to the Code of Conduct and the database Guidelines will help to ensure that research is conducted in accordance with the principles of data protection legislation. In the UK this is encompassed by the Data Protection Act 1998.

Data Protection Definitions

Personal Data means data which relates to a living individual who can be identified

- from the data, or
- from the data and other information in the possession of, or likely to come into the possession of, the data controller

and includes any expression of opinion about the individual and any indication of the intentions of the data controller or any other person in respect of the individual.

Processing means obtaining, recording or holding the information or data or carrying out any operation or set of operations on the information or data, including

- organisation, adaptation or alteration
- retrieval, consultation or use
- disclosure by transmission, dissemination or otherwise making available
- alignment, combination, blocking, erasure or destruction.

It is a requirement of membership that researchers must ensure that their conduct follows the letter and spirit of the principles of Data Protection legislation from the Act. In the UK the eight data protection principles are.

- **The First Principle**
  Personal data shall be processed fairly and lawfully.[1]
- **The Second Principle**
  Personal data shall be obtained only for one or more specified and lawful purposes, and shall not be further processed in any manner incompatible with that purpose or those purposes.
- **The Third Principle**
  Personal data shall be adequate, relevant and not excessive in relation to the purpose or purposes for which they are processed.
- **The Fourth Principle**
  Personal data shall be accurate and, where necessary, kept up to date.
- **The Fifth Principle**
  Personal data processed for any purpose or purposes shall not be kept longer than is necessary for that purpose or those purposes.
- **The Sixth Principle**
  Personal data shall be processed in accordance with the rights of data subjects under this Act.
- **The Seventh Principle**
  Appropriate technical and organisational measures shall be taken against unauthorised or unlawful processing of personal data and against accidental loss or destruction of, or damage to, personal data.
- **The Eighth Principle**
  Personal data shall not be transferred to a country or territory outside the European Economic Area, unless that country or territory ensures an adequate level of protection for the rights and freedoms of data subjects in relation to the processing of personal data.

Exemption for Research Purposes

Where personal data processed for research, statistical or historical purposes are not processed to support decisions affecting particular individuals, or in such a way as likely to cause substantial damage or distress to any data subject, such processing will not breach the Second Principle and the data may be retained indefinitely despite the Fifth Principle.

As long as the results of the research are not published in a form, which identifies any data subject, there is no right of subject access to the data.

Code Definitions

- **Research**

  Research is the collection and analysis of data from a sample of individuals or organisations relating to their characteristics, behaviour, attitudes, opinions or possessions. It includes all forms of marketing and social research such as consumer and industrial surveys, psychological investigations, observational and panel studies.

- **Respondent**

  A respondent is any individual or organisation from whom any information is sought by the researcher for the purpose of a marketing or social research project. The term covers cases where information is to be obtained by verbal interviewing techniques, postal and other self-completion questionnaires, mechanical or electronic equipment, observation and any other method where the identity of the provider of the information may be recorded or otherwise traceable. This includes those approached for research purposes whether or not substantive information is obtained from them and includes those who decline to participate or withdraw at any stage from the research.

- **Interview**

  An interview is any form of contact intended to provide information from a respondent.

- **Identity**

  The identity of a respondent includes, as well as his/her name and/or address, any other information which offers a reasonable chance that he/she can be identified by any of the recipients of the information.

- **Children**

  For the Purpose of the Code, children and young people are defined as those aged under 18. The intention of the provisions regarding age is to protect potentially vulnerable members of society, whatever the source of their vulnerability, and to strengthen the principle of public trust. Consent of a parent or responsible adult should be obtained for interviews with children under 16. Consent must be obtained under the following circumstances:

  – In home/at home (face-to-face and telephone interviewing)

- Group discussions/depth interviews
- Where interviewer and child are alone together.

Interviews being conducted in public places, such as in-street/in-store/central locations, with 14 and 15 years olds may take place without consent if a parent or responsible adult is not accompanying the child. In these situations an explanatory thank you note must be given to the child.

Under special circumstances, a survey may waive parental consent but only with the prior approval of the Professional Standards Committee.

■ **Records**
The term records includes anything containing information relating to a research project and covers all data collection and data processing documents, audio and visual recordings. Primary records are the most comprehensive record of information on which a project is based; they include not only the original data records themselves, but also anything needed to evaluate those records, such as quality control documents. Secondary records are any other records about the Respondent.

■ **Client**
Client includes any individual, organisation, department or division, including any belonging to the same organisation as the research agency which is responsible for commissioning a research project.

■ **Agency**
Agency includes any individual, organisation, department or division, including any belonging to the same organisation as the client which is responsible for, or acts as, a supplier on all or part of a research project.

■ **Professional Body**
Professional body refers to The Market Research Society.

■ **Public Place**
A 'public place' is one to which the public has access (where admission has been gained with or without a charge) and where an individual could reasonably expect to be observed and/or overheard by other people, for example in a shop, in the street or in a place of entertainment.

PRINCIPLES

Research is founded upon the willing co-operation of the public and of business organisations. It depends upon their confidence that it is conducted honestly, objectively, without unwelcome intrusion and without harm to respondents. Its purpose is to collect and analyse information, and not directly to create sales nor to influence the opinions of anyone participating in it. It is in this spirit that the Code of Conduct has been devised.

The general public and other interested parties shall be entitled to complete assurance that every research project is carried out strictly in accordance with this Code, and that their rights of privacy are respected. In particular, they must be assured that no information which could be used to identify them will be made available without their agreement to anyone outside the agency responsible for conducting the research. They must also be assured that the information they supply will not be used for any purposes other than research and that they will not be adversely affected or embarrassed as a direct result of their participation in a research project.

Wherever possible respondents must be informed as to the purpose of the research and the likely length of time necessary for the collection of the information. Finally, the research findings themselves must always be reported accurately and never used to mislead anyone, in any way.

RULES

A. Conditions of Membership and Professional Responsibilities

A.1   Membership of the professional body is granted to individuals who are believed, on the basis of the information they have given, to have such qualifications as are specified from time to time by the professional body and who have undertaken to accept this Code of Conduct. Membership may be withdrawn if this information is found to be inaccurate.

General Responsibilities

A.2   Members shall at all times act honestly in dealings with respondents, clients (actual or potential), employers, employees, subcontractors and the general public.

A.3   Members shall at all times seek to avoid conflicts of interest with clients or employers and shall make prior voluntary and full disclosure to all parties concerned of all matters that might give rise to such conflict.

A.4   The use of letters after an individual's name to indicate membership of The Market Research Society is permitted in the case of Fellows (FMRS) and Full Members (MMRS). All members may point out, where relevant, that they belong to the appropriate category of the professional body.

A.5   Members shall not imply in any statement that they are speaking on behalf of the professional body unless they have the written authority of Council or of some duly delegated individual or committee.

Working Practices

A.6   Members shall ensure that the people (including clients, colleagues and subcontractors) with whom they work are sufficiently familiar with this Code of Conduct and that working arrangements are such that the Code is unlikely to be breached through ignorance of its provisions.

A.7   Members shall not knowingly take advantage, without permission, of the unpublished work of a fellow member which is the property of that member. Specifically, members shall not carry out or commission work based on proposals prepared by a member in another organisation unless permission has been obtained from that organisation.

A.8   All written or oral assurances made by anyone involved in commissioning of conducting projects must be factually correct and honoured.

Responsibilities to Other Members

A.9   Members shall not place other members in a position in which they might unwittingly breach any part of this Code of Conduct.

Responsibilities of Clients to Agencies

A.10 Clients should not normally invite more than four agencies to tender in writing for a project. If they do so, they should disclose how many invitations to tender they are seeking.

A.11 Unless paid for by the client, a specification for a project drawn up by one research agency is the property of that agency and may not be passed on to another agency without the permission of the originating research agency.

Confidential survey research and other activities

(apply B.15 and Notes to B.15)

A.12 Members shall only use the term *confidential survey research* to describe research projects which are based upon respondent anonymity and do not involve the divulgence of identities or personal details of respondents to others except for research purposes.

A.13 If any of the following activities are involved in, or form part of, a project then the project lies outside the scope of confidential survey research and must not be described or presented as such:

(a) enquiries whose objectives include obtaining personal information about private individuals per se, whether for legal, political, supervisory (e.g. job performance), private or other purposes:

(b) the acquisition of information for use by credit-rating or similar purposes;

(c) the compilation, updating or enhancement of lists, registers or databases which are not exclusively for research purpose (e.g. which will be used for direct or relationship marketing);

(d) industrial, commercial or any other form of espionage;

(e) sales or promotional responses to individual respondents;

(f) the collection of debts;

(g) fund raising;

(h) direct or indirect attempts, including the framing of questions, to influence a respondent's opinions or attitudes on any issue other than for experimental purposes which are identified in any report or publication of the results.

A.14 Where any such activities referred to by paragraph A.13 are carried out by a member, the member must clearly differentiate such activities by:

(a) not describing them to anyone as confidential survey research and

(b) making it clear to respondents at the start of any data collection exercise what the purposes of the activity are and that the activity is not confidential survey research.

Scope of code

A.15 When undertaking confidential survey research based on respondent anonymity, members shall abide by the ICC/ESOMAR International Code of Conduct which constitutes Section B of this Code.

A.16 MRS Guidelines issued, other than those published as consultative drafts, are binding on members where they indicate that actions or procedures *shall or must* be adhered to by members. Breaches of these conditions will be treated as breaches of the Code and may be subject to disciplinary action.

A.17 Recommendations within such guidelines that members should behave in certain ways are advisory only.

A.18 It is the responsibility of members to keep themselves updated on changes or amendments to any part of this Code which are published from time to time and announced in publications and on the web pages of the Society. If in doubt about the interpretation of the Code, members may consult the Professional Standards Committee or its Codeline Service set up to deal with Code enquiries.

Disciplinary action

A.19 Complaints regarding breaches of the Code of Conduct by those in membership of the MRS must be made to The Market Research Society.

A.20 Membership may be withdrawn, or other disciplinary action taken, if, on investigation of a complaint, it is found that in the opinion of the professional body, any part of the member's research work or behaviour breaches this Code of Conduct.

A.21 Members must make available the necessary information as and when requested by the Professional Standards Committee and Disciplinary Committee in the course of an enquiry.

A.22 Membership may be withdrawn, or other disciplinary action taken, if a member is deemed guilty of unprofessional conduct. This is defined as a member:

(a) being guilty of any act or conduct which in the opinion of a body appointed by Council might bring discredit on the profession, the professional body or its members;

(b) being guilty of any breach of the Code of Conduct set out in this document;

(c) knowingly being in breach of any other regulations laid down from time to time by the Council of the professional body;

(d) failing without good reason to assist the professional body in the investigation of a complaint;

(e) having a receiving order made against him/her or making any arrangement or composition with his/her creditors;

(f) being found to be in breach of the Data Protection Act by the Data Protection Registrar.

A.23 No member will have his/her membership withdrawn, demoted or suspended under this Code without an opportunity of a hearing before a tribunal, of which s/he will have at least one month's notice.

A.24 Normally, the MRS will publish the names of members who have their membership withdrawn, demoted or are suspended or have other disciplinary action taken with the reasons for the decision.

A.25 If a member subject to a complaint resigns his/her membership of the Society whilst the case is unresolved, then such resignation shall be published and in the event of re-admission to membership the member shall be required to co-operate in the completion of any outstanding disciplinary process.

B. ICC/ESOMAR Code of Marketing and Social Research Practice

General

B.1   Marketing research must always be carried out objectively and in accordance with established scientific principles.

B.2   Marketing research must always conform to the national and international legislation which applies in those countries involved in a given research project.

The rights of respondents

B.3   Respondents' co-operation in a marketing research project is entirely voluntary at all stages. They must not be misled when being asked for co-operation.

B.4   Respondents' anonymity must be strictly preserved. If the respondent on request from the Researcher has given permission for data to be passed on in a form which allows that respondent to be identified personally:

(a)   the Respondent must first have been told to whom the information would be supplied and the purposes for which it will be used, and also

(b)   the Respondent must ensure that the information will not be used for any non-research purpose and that the recipient of the information has agreed to conform to the requirements of the Code.

B.5   The Researcher must take all reasonable precautions to ensure that Respondents are in no way directly harmed or adversely affected as a result of their participation in a marketing research project.

B.6   The Researcher must take special care when interviewing children and young people. The informed consent of the parent or responsible adult must first be obtained for interviews with children.

B.7   Respondents must be told (normally at the beginning of the interview) if observation techniques or recording equipment are used, except where these are used in a public place. If a respondent so wishes, the record or relevant section of it must be destroyed or deleted. Respondents' anonymity must not be infringed by the use of such methods.

B.8 Respondents must be enabled to check without difficulty the identity and bona fides of the Researcher.

The professional responsibilities of researchers

B.9 Researchers must not, whether knowingly or negligently, act in any way which could bring discredit on the marketing research profession or lead to a loss of public confidence in it.

B.10 Researchers must not make false claims about their skills and experience or about those of their organisation.

B.11 Researchers must not unjustifiably criticise or disparage other Researchers.

B.12 Researchers must always strive to design research which is cost-efficient and of adequate quality, and then to carry this out to the specification agreed with the Client.

B.13 Researchers must ensure the security of all research records in their possession.

B.14 Researchers must not knowingly allow the dissemination of conclusions from a marketing research project which are not adequately supported by the data. They must always be pre-pared to make available the technical information necessary to assess the validity of any published findings.

B.15 When acting in their capacity as Researchers the latter must not undertake any non-research activities, for example database marketing involving data about individuals which will be used for direct marketing and promotional activities. Any such non-research activities must always, in the way they are organised and carried out, be clearly differentiated from marketing research activities.

Mutual rights and responsibilities of researchers and clients

B.16 These rights and responsibilities will normally be governed by a written Contract between the Researcher and the Client. The parties may amend the provisions of rules B.19 – B.23 below if they have agreed this in writing beforehand; but the other requirements of this Code may not be altered in this way. Marketing research must also always be conducted according to the principles of fair competition, as generally understood and accepted.

B.17 The Researcher must inform the Client if the work to be carried out for that Client is to be combined or syndicated in the same project with work for other Clients but must not disclose the identity of such clients without their permission.

B.18 The Researcher must inform the Client as soon as possible in advance when any part of the work for that Client is to be subcontracted outside the Researcher's own organisation (including the use of any outside consultants). On request the Client must be told the identity of any such subcontractor.

B.19 The Client does not have the right, without prior agreement between the parties involved, to exclusive use of the Researcher's services or those of his organisation, whether in whole or in part. In carrying out work for different clients, however, the Researcher must endeavour to avoid possible clashes of interest between the services provided to those clients.

B.20 The following Records remain the property of the Client and must not be disclosed by the Researcher to any third party without the Client's permission:

(a) marketing research briefs, specifications and other information provided by the Client;

(b) the research data and findings from a marketing research project (except in the case of syndicated or multi-client projects or services where the same data are available to more than one client.

The Client has, however, no right to know the names or addresses of Respondents unless the latter's explicit permission for this has first been obtained by the Researcher (this particular requirement cannot be altered under Rule B.16).

B.21 Unless it is specifically agreed to the contrary, the following Records remain the property of the Researcher:

(a) marketing research proposals and cost quotations (unless these have been paid for by the Client). They must not be disclosed by the Client to any third party, other than to a consultant working for the Client on that project (with the exception of any consultant working also for a competitor of the Researcher). In particular, they must not be used by the Client to influence research proposals or cost quotations from other Researchers.

(b) the contents of a report in the case of syndicated research and/or multi-client projects or services when the same data are available to more than one client and where it is clearly understood that the resulting reports are available for general purchase or subscription. The Client may not disclose the findings of such research to any third party (other than his own consultants and advisors for use in connection with his business) without the permission of the Researcher.

(c) all other research Records prepared by the Researcher (with the exception in the case of non-syndicated projects of the report to the Client, and also the research design and questionnaire where the costs of developing these are covered by the charges paid by the Client).

B.22 The Researcher must conform to current agreed professional practice relating to the keeping of such records for an appropriate period of time after the end of the project. On request the Researcher must supply the Client with duplicate copies of such records provided that such duplicates do not breach anonymity and confidentiality requirements (Rule B.4); that the request is made within the agreed time limit for keeping the Records; and that the Client pays the reasonable costs of providing the duplicates.

B.23 The Researcher must not disclose the identity of the Client (provided there is no legal obligation to do so) or any confidential information about the latter's business, to any third party without the Client's permission.

B.24 The Researcher must, on request, allow the Client to arrange for checks on the quality of fieldwork and data preparation provided that the Client pays any additional costs involved in this. Any such checks must conform to the requirements of Rule B.4.

B.25 The Researcher must provide the Client with all appropriate technical details of any research project carried out for that Client.

B.26 When reporting on the results of a marketing research project the Researcher must make a clear distinction between the findings as such, the Researcher's interpretation of these and any recommendations based on them.

B.27 Where any of the findings of a research project are published by the Client, the latter has a responsibility to ensure that these are not misleading. The Researcher must be consulted and agree in advance the form and content of publication, and must take action to correct any misleading statements about the research and its findings.

B.28 Researchers must not allow their names to be used in connection with any research project as an assurance that the latter has been carried out in conformity with this Code unless they are confident that the project has in all respects met the Code's requirements.

B.29 Researchers must ensure that Clients are aware of the existence of this Code and of the need to comply with its requirements.

NOTES

How the ICC/ESOMAR International Code of Marketing and Social Research Practice should be Applied

These general notes published by ICC/ESOMAR apply to the interpretation of Section B of this Code in the absence of any specific interpretation which may be found in the MRS Definitions, in Part A of the MRS Code or in Guidelines published by the MRS. MRS members who are also members of ESOMAR will in addition be subject to requirements of the guidelines published by ESOMAR.

These Notes are intended to help users of the Code to interpret and apply it in practice.

The Notes, and the Guidelines referred to in them, will be reviewed and reissued from time to time. Any query or problem about how to apply the Code in a specific situation should be addressed to the Secretariat of MRS.

The Rights of Respondents

All Respondents entitled to be sure that when they agree to co-operate in any marketing research project they are fully protected by the provisions of this Code and that the Researcher will conform to its requirements. This applies equally to Respondents interviewed as private individuals and to those interviewed as representatives of organisations of different kinds.

Note on Rule B.3

Researcher and those working on their behalf (e.g. interviewers) must not, in order to secure Respondents' co-operation, make statements or promises which are knowingly misleading or incorrect – for example, about the likely length of the interview or about the possibilities of being re-interviewed on a later occasion. Any such statements and assurances given to Respondents must be fully honoured.

Respondents are entitled to withdraw from an interview at any stage and to refuse to co-operate further in the research project. Any or all of the information collected from or about them must be destroyed without delay if the Respondents so request.

Note on Rule B.4

All indications of the identity of Respondents should be physically separated from the records of the information they have provided as soon as possible after the completion of any necessary fieldwork quality checks. The Researcher must ensure that any information which might identify Respondents is stored securely, and separately from the other information they have provided; and that access to such material is restricted to authorised research personnel within the Researcher's own organisation for specific research purposes (e.g. field administration, data processing, panel or 'longitudinal' studies or other forms of research involving recall interviews).

To preserve Respondents' anonymity not only their names and addresses but also any other information provided by or about them which could in practice identify them (e.g. their Company and job title) must be safeguarded.

These anonymity requirements may be relaxed only under the following safeguards:

(a) Where the Respondent has given explicit permission for this under the conditions of 'informed consent' summarised in Rule 4 (a) and (b).

(b) where disclosure of names to a third party (e.g. a Subcontractor) is essential for any research purpose such as data processing or further interview (e.g. an independent fieldwork quality check) or for further follow-up research. The original Researcher is responsible for ensuring that any such third party agrees to observe the requirements of this Code, in writing, if the third party has not already formally subscribed to the Code.

It must be noted that even these limited relaxations may not be permissible in certain countries. The definition of 'non-research activity', referred to in Rule 4(b), is dealt with in connection with Rule 15.

Note on Rule B.5

The Researcher must explicitly agree with the Client arrangements regarding the responsibilities for product safety and for dealing with any complaints or damage arising from faulty products or product misuse. Such responsibilities will normally rest with the Client, but the Researcher must ensure that products are correctly stored and handled while in the Researcher's charge and that Respondents are given appropriate instructions for their use. More generally, Researchers should avoid interviewing at inappropriate or inconvenient times. They should also avoid the use of unnecessarily long interviews; and the asking of personal questions which may worry or annoy Respondents, unless the information is essential to the purposes of the study and the reasons for needing it are explained to the Respondent.

Note on Rule B.6

The definitions of 'children' and 'young people' may vary by country but if not otherwise specified locally should be taken as 'under 14 years' and '14–17 years' (under 16, and 16–17 respectively in the UK).

Note on Rule B.7

The Respondent should be told at the beginning of the interview that recording techniques are to be used unless this knowledge might bias the Respondent's subsequent behaviour: in such cases the Respondent must be told about the recording at the end of the interview and be given the opportunity to see or hear the relevant section of the record and, if they so wish, to have this destroyed. A 'public place' is defined as one to which the public has free access and where an individual could reasonably expect to be observed and/or overheard by other people present, for example in a shop or in the street.

Note on Rule B.8

The name and address/telephone number of the Researcher must normally be made available to the Respondent at the time of interview. In cases where an accommodation address or 'cover name' are used for data collection purposes arrangements must be made to enable Respondents subsequently to find without difficulty or avoidable expense the name and address of the Researcher. Wherever possible 'Freephone' or similar facilities should be provided so that Respondents can check the Researcher's bona fides without cost to themselves.

The professional responsibilities of researchers

This Code is not intended to restrict the rights of Researchers to undertake any legitimate marketing research activity and to operate competitively in so doing. However, it is essential that in pursuing these objectives the general public's confidence in the integrity of marketing research is not undermined in any way. This Section sets out the responsibilities which the Researcher has towards the public at large and towards the marketing research profession and other members of this.

Note on Rule B.14

The kinds of technical information which should on request be made available include those listed in the Notes to Rule B.25. The Researcher must not however disclose information which is confidential to the Client's business, nor need he/she disclose information relating to parts of the survey which were not published.

Note on Rule B.15

The kinds of non-research activity which must not be associated in any way with the carrying out of marketing research include:

enquiries whose objectives are to obtain personal information about private individuals per se, whether for legal, political, supervisory (e.g. job performance), private or other purposes; the acquisition of information for use for credit-rating or similar purposes; the compilation, updating or enhancement of lists, registers or databases which are not exclusively for research purposes (e.g. which will be used for direct marketing); industrial, commercial or any other form of espionage; sales or promotional attempts to individual Respondents; the collection of debts; fund-raising; direct or indirect attempts, including by the design of the questionnaire, to influence a Respondent's opinions, attitudes or behaviour on any issue.

Certain of these activities – in particular the collection of information for databases for subsequent use in direct marketing and similar operations – are legitimate marketing activities in their own right. Researchers (especially those working within a client company) may often be involved with such activities, directly or indirectly. In such cases it is essential that a clear distinction is made between these activities and marketing research since by definition marketing research anonymity rules cannot be applied to them.

Situations may arise where a Researcher wishes, quite legitimately, to become involved with marketing database work for direct marketing (as distinct from marketing research) purposes: such work must not be carried out under the name of marketing research or of a marketing research Organisation as such.

The mutual rights and responsibilities of researchers and clients

This Code is not intended to regulate the details of business relationships between Researchers and Clients except in so far as these may involve principles of general interest and concern. Most such matters should be regulated by the individual business. It is clearly vital that such Contracts are based on an adequate understanding and consideration of the issues involved.

Note on Rule B.18

Although it is usually known in advance what subcontractors will be used, occasions do arise during the project where subcontractors need to be brought in, or changed, at very short notice. In such cases, rather than cause delays to the project in order to inform the Client it will usually be sensible and acceptable to let the Client know as quickly as possible after the decision has been taken.

Note on Rule B.22

The period of time for which research Records should be kept by the Researcher will vary with the nature of the project (e.g. ad hoc, panel, repetitive) and the possible requirements for follow-up research or further analysis. It will normally be longer for the stored research data resulting from a survey (tabulations, discs, tapes etc.) than for primary field records (the original completed questionnaires and similar basic records). The period must be disclosed to, and agreed by, the Client in advance. In default of any agreement to the contrary, in the case of ad hoc surveys the normal period for which the primary field records should be retained is one year after completion of the fieldwork while the research data should be stored for possible further analysis for at least two years. The Researcher should take suitable precautions to guard against any accidental loss of the information, whether stored physically or electronically, during the agreed storage period.

Note on Rule B.24

On request the Client, or his mutually acceptable representative, may observe a limited number of interviews for this purpose. In certain cases, such as panels or in situations where a Respondent might be known to (or be in subsequent contact with) the Client, this may require the previous agreement of the Respondent. Any such observer must agree to be bound by the provisions of this Code, especially Rule B.4.

The Researcher is entitled to be recompensed for any delays and increased fieldwork costs which may result from such a request. The Client must be informed if the observation of interviews may mean that the results of such interviews will need to be excluded from the overall survey analysis because they are no longer methodologically comparable.

In the case of multi-client studies the Researcher may require that any such observer is independent of any of the Clients.

Where an independent check on the quality of the fieldwork is to be carried out by a different research agency the latter must conform in all respects to the requirements of this Code. In particular, the anonymity of the original Respondents must be fully safeguarded and their names and addresses used exclusively for the purposes of back-checks, not being disclosed to the Client. Similar considerations apply where the Client wishes to carry out checks on the quality of data preparation work.

Notes on Rule B.25

The Client is entitled to the following information about any marketing research project to which he has subscribed:

(1) Background

- for whom the study was conducted
- the purpose of the study
- names of subcontractors and consultants performing any substantial part of the work

(2) Sample

- a description of the intended and actual universe covered
- the size, nature and geographical distribution of the sample (both planned and achieved); and where relevant, the extent to which any of the data collected were obtained from only part of the sample
- details of the sampling method and any weighting methods used
- where technically relevant, a statement of response rates and a discussion of any possible bias due to non-response

(3) Data collection

- a description of the method by which the information was collected
- a description of the field staff, briefing and field quality control methods used
- the method of recruiting Respondents; and the general nature of any incentives offered to secure their co-operation
- when the fieldwork was carried out
- (in the case of 'desk research') a clear statement of the sources of the information and their likely reliability

(4) Presentation of results

- the relevant factual findings obtained

- bases of percentages (both weighted and unweighted)
- general indications of the probable statistical margins of error to be attached to the main findings, and the levels of statistical significance of differences between key figures
- the questionnaire and other relevant documents and materials used (or, in the case of a shared project, that portion relating to the matter reported on).

The Report on a project should normally cover the above points or provide a reference to a readily available document which contains the information.

Note on Rule B.27

If the Client does not consult and agree in advance the form of publication with the Researcher the latter is entitled to:

(a) refuse permission for his name to be used in connection with the published findings and
(b) publish the appropriate technical details of the project (as listed in the Notes to B.25).

Note on Rule B.29

It is recommended that Researchers specify in their research proposals that they follow the requirements of this Code and that they make a copy available to the Client if the latter does not already have one.

CODELINE

Codeline is a free, confidential answer service to Market Research Society Code of Conduct related queries raised by market researchers, clients, respondents and other interested parties. The aim of Codeline is to provide an immediate, personal and practical interpretation and advice service.

Codeline is directly responsible to the MRS Professional Standards Committee (PSC) to which each query and its response is reported at PSC's next meeting. Queries from enquirers are handled by an individual member of the Codeline panel, drawn from past members of the

PSC. As long as contact can be made with the enquirer, queries will be dealt with by Codeline generally within 24 hours. Where necessary, the responding Codeline member can seek further specialist advice.

Codeline's response to enquirers is not intended to be definitive but is the personal interpretation of the individual Codeline member, based on personal Code-related experience. PSC and Codeline panellists may highlight some of the queries and responses for examination and ratification by the PSC, the ultimate arbiter of the Code, at its next meeting. In the event that an individual Codeline response is not accepted by the PSC the enquirer will be notified immediately.

Enquirer details are treated as totally confidential outside the PSC but should 'Research' or any other MRS journal wish to refer to a particularly interesting or relevant query in 'Problem Page' or similar, permission is sought and obtained from the enquirer before anonymous publication and after that query's examination by PSC.

Codeline operates in the firm belief that a wide discussion of the issues arising from queries or anomalies in applying the Code and its associated guidelines within the profession will lead both to better understanding, awareness and application of the Code among members and to a better public appreciation of the ethical standards the market research industry professes and to which it aspires.

How to use Codeline

Codeline deals with any market research ethical issues. To contact Codeline please phone or fax the MRS Secretariat who will then allocate your query to a Codeline panellist.

If you choose to contact MRS by phone, the MRS Secretariat will ask you to confirm by fax the nature of your query, whether or not the caller is an MRS member or works for an organisation which employs an MRS member and a phone number at which you can be contacted. This fax will then be sent to the allocated panellist who will discuss your query directly with you by phone as soon as possible after receipt of your enquiry.

Please forward any queries about the MRS Code of Conduct and Guidelines, in writing to the:

MRS Secretariat, 15 Northburgh Street, London EC1V OJR

Tel: 020 7490 4911 Fax: 020 7490 0608

NOTES

[1]In particular shall not be processed unless at least one of the conditions in Schedule 2 is met, and in the case of sensitive data, at least one of the conditions of Schedule 3 is also met. (These schedules provide that in determining whether personal data has been processed fairly, consideration must be given to the basis on which it was obtained.)

Glossary of market research terms

It is always of concern to management that the advertising, research and computer sectors are full of jargon. You have to be in the knowledge to be able to use this jargon, and if used incorrectly it can almost contribute to your becoming alienated and not accepted among the users of the specialist techniques. Therefore, I felt it worthwhile to list the key research jargon and to identify the usefulness of the techniques described. This glossary, therefore, is the key checklist of everything a manager must know in order to use and perform with research effectively – and be seen to be 'in the know-how' of research.

Attitude statements   A psychological concept designed to evaluate and investigate values, beliefs and motives for different forms of behaviour. Developing statements to describe your company and its products and services compared with those of your competitors provides the means of creating a control, asking consumers whether they agree or disagree with the attitudes and, in time, monitoring the changes.

Cluster analysis   A technique of multivariate analysis, which identifies groups of individuals that are similar to and different from each other. It is a way of establishing whether a group of people have similar attitudes or characteristics, which help to define or confirm subsegments of a market. It is an important technique for defining which types of product suit different types of consumer, and also establishing whether communications can be developed for specific market segments.

Conjoint analysis   A method of evaluating consumer preferences among product concepts, which vary in respect of several attributes, based on asking people to rank those they most and least prefer. Using this analysis helps to develop data on how certain types of customer have a preference for purchasing and using certain types of product. It will therefore define what is the ideal product for customers because of how well the product meets their needs.

Demographics   Sex, age and social grade are the key parts of the classification data in research, and comprise the demographics of the market being researched. It is vital for defining a market initially to know who are the current and potential customers. This becomes the basic benchmark data on which psychographic analyses are developed and created. The Market Research Society published the 5th Edition of *Occupations Groupings: A Job Dictionary* in 2002 (ISBN 0–9061–1727–5). The following is extracted as the key information for survey users:

Occupation Groups
The Occupation Groups are as follows:

A   Approximately 3% of the total population. These are professional people, very senior managers in business or commerce or top-level civil servants. Retired people, previously grade A, and their widows.

B   Approximately 20% of the population. Middle management executives in large organizations, with appropriate qualifications. Principal officers in local government and civil service. Top management or owners of small business concerns, educational and service establishments. Retired people, previously grade B, and their widows.

C1 Approximately 28% of the total population. Junior management, owners of small establishments, and all others in non-manual positions. Jobs in this group have very varied responsibilities and educational requirements. Retired people, previously grade C1 and their widows.

C2 Approximately 21% of the population. All skilled manual workers, and those manual workers with responsibility for other people. Retired people, previously C2, with pensions from their job. Widows, if receiving pensions from their late husband's job.

D   Approximately 18% of the population. All semi-skilled and unskilled manual workers, apprentices and trainees to skilled workers. Retired

people, previously grade D, with pensions from their job. Widows, if
receiving a pension from their late husband's job.

E   Approximately 10% of the population. All those entirely dependent
on the state long-term, through sickness, unemployment, old age or
other reasons. Those unemployed for a period exceeding six months.
Casual workers and those without a regular income. Only households without a Chief Income Earner will be coded in this group.

Grading on Occupation

In the majority of cases, the decision as to whose occupation to use for
grading is very simple.

- Social grading based on occupation of Head of Household, or
- Social grading based on Chief Income Earner.

Desk research   This is based on the use of secondary data, collecting
published information relevant to the company's markets and
products. Collection of this information may be important in
understanding markets and can help to design survey research,
in particular to prevent the survey duplicating the collection of data
that is already available.

Family life cycles   Stages in the development of families: young
single people and young couples, the early stage; couples with children at home, the mid-life stage; and older people without children,
the late stage.

Forecasting   Estimating the probability of an event in the future. It
may also be a prediction mode using a mathematical model, or
from an extrapolation of current trends. This is important as a technique in a defined market, which can be tracked by monitoring key
facts, habits and activities of the market that has been classified. It
is particularly useful as a way of analysing products and product
performances if product design or formulation is changed to alter
the market or sales in the market.

Geodemographics   A method of classifying households based on
multivariate analysis of data from the Census of Population. The
practical application of geodemographic classifications generally
depends on computer matching addresses to district classifications
by means of the postcode. The application of geodemographics is
useful for direct marketing, retail planning, or developing promotions and specific marketing activities for monitoring markets or
ethnic groups.

Image statements Consumers' perceptions or impressions of a company, product or service expressed in a clear statement. These are used to establish how close to or far away its ideas, concepts and strategies are from consumer needs.

Market mapping A 'map' which shows the relative positions of the products in the market, consumers' or consumer characteristics. It is the most effective method for summarizing the findings of attitude research. There are two applications for market mapping. The first is literally to draw up the structure of the market and to add to the map the facts about each level of the market: the volume of sales, the classification of the customer types and so on. It is particularly good for understanding a market more clearly. The second is to use the analysis of survey research and to plot on a map the relationship between the defined customer types and the way in which attitudes are described or product attributes are rated. It is good for developing a product or communications strategy in sophisticated markets where it is important to develop strategies to respond to consumers' changing and demanding needs to counter competitive threats.

Market segmentation Using classifications or market facts to divide a market into the characteristics of the product or service, user and buyer in the market, type or size of company. A central and very important marketing technique, market segmentation is a key tool to making research useful to grow business. It allows customer types and their different needs to be analysed, interpreted and monitored effectively. It assists in understanding how the market divides and how customers behave in different ways with different needs.

Marketing information system All the information available to management, together with the hardware for its storage, processing and retrieval. Market intelligence, reports from all departments and market research are all part of this system. Creating, using and monitoring such a system is important for making the organization customer oriented.

Modelling A model is a summary of observations, including mathematical models. It is a way of imitating or copying the market forces and testing out changes in a market, then observing the effects that result. It is a technique that is particularly effective in product and service research. It helps to anticipate market changes and move quickly once the effects of competitors' activity are reanalysed in the model.

Multivariate techniques   Those techniques that examine the relationships among a number of variables. They include analysis of variance, multi-regression, factor and principal component analysis, cluster analysis and discriminant analysis. Application of these techniques to survey analysis provides the manager with the opportunity to advance product and communications planning. It helps to translate the methods of marketing into the language and behaviour of consumers.

Paired comparison test   A test to compare two products or samples, with the purpose of getting a user or buyer to discriminate between them or identify changes or improvements. It is an important way of developing data to identify users' and buyers' attitudes to competitors' products and establish consumers' perceived benefits of your own.

Psychographic analysis   A segmentation application that classifies people into groups based on their behaviour or attitudes. It is becoming more and more important as a technique as it helps to classify and group the customers in a market, reflecting their needs in the context of their preferences and buying habits. It helps to make communications more direct and relevant, and to make market analysis more realistic in the context of getting to know the customer.

Regression analysis   A statistical method of calculating an equation which is applied to a set of bivariate or multivariate observations. It is a useful technique for analysing different market segments to identify whether any of the subgroups of customer have any similarities in behaviour, attitudes or preferences.

Sample   A representation of the whole, whose purpose is to enable investigation of the characteristics of the population. It is comprised of parts or subsets of the population being researched. Survey research depends on getting this right, as a survey completed with the wrong type of population is worthless.

Sampling   The technique for selecting a sample. It depends on setting up a sampling frame and identifying sampling units, which comprise a population. Survey research is only successful if this is completed well.

Trade-off models   A technique to discover the most attractive combination of attributes for a product or service, by the respondent expressing a preference for one or other alternative. An important technique for understanding clearly why people buy, how they evaluate whether the product or service that is offered corresponds with their needs, and the way in which they decide on making the purchase.

References

Aaker, D (1996) *Building Strong Brands*, Free Press, New York

Adams, M (2000) CRM is not enough for an effective business strategy, *Knowledge Management*, Nov

Alexander, M (2000) Codes and contexts: practical semiotics for the qualitative researcher, paper presented at the Market Research Society Conference

Anshuetz, N (1997) Point of view: brand popularity: the myth of segmenting to brand success, *Journal of Advertising Research*, **37** (1)

Baker, K and McDonald, C (1999) Importance measure: a review, paper presented at the Market Research Society Conference

Baker, T and Callingham, M (2003) Market research at the high table: defining the need and plotting the route, paper presented at the Market Research Society Conference

Barnham, C (1995) Does size count?, paper given at the AQRP Trends Day

Brand, C and Jarvis, S (2000) Mind games: the psychology of research, paper presented at the Market Research Society Conference

Brooker, S and Cawson, P (2001) The prevalence of child abuse and neglect: a survey of young people, paper presented at the Market Research Society Conference

Callingham, M (1991) The role of qualitative notions in company decision making, *Journal of the Market Research Society*, **33** (1)

Callingham, M and Baker, T (2001) An innovative unified brand and market measurement system for strategic investment decisions, paper presented at the Market Research Society Conference

Callingham, M and Baker, T (2002) We know what you they think, but do we know what they do?, paper presented at the Market Research Society Conference

Catterall, M (2001) Private communication

Chandler, J and Owen, M (1989) Genesis to Revelation: the evolution of qualitative philosophy, paper presented at the Market Research Society Conference

Coates, J (1998) Building consumer insight: researching things for life, paper presented at the Market Research Society Conference

Collins, M (1989) Quant is overly deductive: concepts of accuracy in market research, paper presented to a one-day seminar on Reliability and Validity in Market Research

Cowan, D (1994) Good information, generals cannot do without it: why do CEOs think that they can? *Marketing Intelligence and Planning*, **12** (11)

Docherty, D and Morrison, D (1990) Citizenship: morality and broadcasting, paper presented at the Market Research Society Conference

Downham, J (1993) *BMRB International: The first sixty years*, BRMB International, London

Dugdale, M (1969) *My Statistics are Vital*, Educational Explorers, Reading, UK

Ehrenberg, A, Long, S and Kennedy, R (2000) Competitive brands: user-profiles hardly differ, paper presented at the Market Research Society Conference

Feldwick, P (1996) What is brand equity anyway and how do you measure it?, paper presented at the Market Research Society Conference

Fisher, Susie (2000) Museums, galleries and the arts world, in *Qualitative Research in Context*, ed L Marks, Chapter 9, Admap Publications, Henley-on-Thames

Fletcher, J and Morgan, W (2000) New directions in qualitative brand research, paper presented at the Market Research Society Conference

Gabriel C (1990) The validity of qualitative market research, *Journal of the Market Research Society*, **32** (4)

Goodwin, P and Wright, G (1997) *Decision Management for Management Judgement*, Wiley, Chichester

Goodyear, M (1996) Divided by a common language: diversity and deception in the world of global marketing, paper presented at the Market Research Society Conference

Gordon, W (1999) Private communication

Hall, N (ed) (1993) *Exploring Chaos: A guide to the new science of disorder*, W W Norton, New York

Hammond, J S (1998) The hidden traps in decision making, *Harvard Business Review*, Sept/Oct

Hannah, M and Brand, C (1999) Do customer satisfaction programmes satisfy the dissatisfied?, paper presented at the Market Research Society Conference

Harrison, J and Ingledew, S (1988) Issues in and approaches to international research, paper presented at the Market Research Society Conference

Harvey, D (1995) *The Condition of Post-Modernity*, Blackwell, Oxford

Hedges, A and Duncan, S (2000) Qualitative research in the social policy field, in *Qualitative Research in Context*, ed L Marks, Admap Publications, Henley-on-Thames

Hitching, C and Stone, D (1988) *Understanding Accounting*, Pitman, London

Hussey, J and Hussey, R (1997) *Business Research*, Macmillan Business, Basingstoke

Imms, M (1999) A reassessment of the roots and the theoretical basis of qualitative market research in the UK, paper presented at the Market Research Society Conference

Imms, M (2001) Private communication

Krabuanrat, K and Phelps, R (1998) Heuristics and rationality in strategic decision making: an exploratory study, *Journal of Business Research*

Kuhn, T (1962) *The Structure of Scientific Revolutions*, University of Chicago Press, Chicago

Levitt, T (1981) Marketing intangible products and product intangibles, *Harvard Business Review*, May/Jun

Lewis, J and White, C (1999) Appraising the role of citizens' juries, paper presented at the Market Research Society Conference

Lovell, N and Henderson, F (2000) Come together: increasing popular involvement in local decision making, paper presented at the Market Research Society Conference

Lovett, P (2001) Ethics shmethics! as long as you get the next job: a moral dilemma, paper presented at the Market Research Society Conference

Martensson, M (2000) A critical review of knowledge management as a management tool, *Journal of Knowledge Management*, **4** (3)

Mattinson, D (1998) People power in politics, paper presented at the Market Research Society Conference

Mattinson, D and Bell, T (2000) Politics and qualitative research, in *Qualitative Research in Context*, ed L Marks, Admap Publications, Henley-on-Thames

Mitchel Waldrop, M (1994) *Complexity: The emerging science at the edge of order and chaos*, Penguin, Harmondsworth

Morris, A (1996) Descended from the same stock?, paper presented at the BIG Conference

Morris, A (2001) Private communication

Nonka, I and Takeeuchi, H (1995) *The Knowledge-Creating Company*, Oxford University Press, Oxford

Pawles, J (1999) Mining the international consumer, *Journal of the Market Research Society*, **41** (1)

Perrott, N (1998) Piecing together the jigsaw: how research fits into the strategy picture, paper presented at the Market Research Society Conference

Pyke, A (2000) It's all in the brief, paper presented at the Market Research Society Conference

Quinn Patton, M (1986). Validity and reliability utilisation: focused evaluation, Sage, Chapter 8

Rigg, M (2003) Private communication

Robson, S and Hedges, A (1993) Analysis and interpretation of qualitative findings, Report of the Qualitative Interest Group of the Market Research Society

Robson, S and Ballard, A (2000) Qualitative research in the development of higher education, in *Qualitative Research in Context*, ed L Marks, Admap Publications, Henley-on-Thames

Shaw, R and Edwards, A (2000) What do planners want from research? Not 'the truth'?, paper presented at the Market Research Society Conference

Shields, G (2001) Meeting the needs of actionable consumer insight: the Scottish Courage perspective, paper presented at the Market Research Society Conference

Simmons, S and Lovejoy, A (2003) Oh no, the consultants are coming, paper presented at the Market Research Society Conference

Smith, D and Fletcher, J (1999) Going the extra mile: putting the markets researchers in the decision makers shoes, paper presented at the Market Research Society Conference

Spackman, N and Barker, A (2000) Happy Millennium: a research paradigm for the twenty-first century, paper presented at the Market Research Society Conference

Sykes W (1990) Validity and reliability in qualitative market research: a review of the literature, *Journal of the Market Research Society*, **32** (3)

Wardle, J (2001) Private communication

Index

The Market Research Society

With over 8,000 members in more than 50 countries, The Market Research Society (MRS) is the world's largest international membership organization for professional researchers and others engaged in (or interested in) market, social and opinion research.

It has a diverse membership of individual researchers within agencies, independent consultancies, client-side organisations, and the academic community – at all levels of seniority and in all job functions.

All MRS members agree to comply with the MRS Code of Conduct (see Appendix), which is supported by the Codeline advisory service and a range of specialist guidelines on best practice.

MRS offers various qualifications and membership grades, as well as training and professional development resources to support these. It is the official awarding body in the UK for vocational qualifications in market research.

MRS is a major supplier of publications and information services, conferences and seminars, and many other meeting and networking opportunities for researchers.

MRS is 'the voice of the profession' in its media relations and public affairs activities on behalf of professional research practitioners, and aims to achieve the most favourable climate of opinion and legislative environment for research.

The Market Research Society (Limited by Guarantee) Company Number 518685

Company Information: Registered office and business address:
15 Northburgh Street, London EC1V OJR
Telephone: 020 7490 4911
Fax: 020 7490 0608
e-mail: info@marketresearch.org.uk
Web site: www.mrs.org.uk